FUTURE PEACE

FUTURE PEACE

TECHNOLOGY, AGGRESSION, AND THE RUSH TO WAR

———————•———————

ROBERT H. LATIFF

University of Notre Dame Press
Notre Dame, Indiana

University of Notre Dame Press
Notre Dame, Indiana 46556
undpress.nd.edu

Copyright © 2022 by the University of Notre Dame

Published in the United States of America

Library of Congress Control Number: 2021948498

ISBN: 978-0-268-20189-0 (Hardback)
ISBN: 978-0-268-20191-3 (WebPDF)
ISBN: 978-0-268-20188-3 (Epub)

For Dale

All war is a symptom of man's failure as a thinking animal.

—John Steinbeck, *Once There Was a War*, 1943

CONTENTS

PREFACE

Americans are fascinated by new technologies and advanced weapons, and the American way of war has long been built around reliance on technological superiority. However, citizens and most political leaders have precious little understanding of those technologies and no more than a passing interest in the complex issues of foreign policy and military affairs. This combination of characteristics leads to an uninformed embrace of military power that may well create a dangerous situation where we think that all conflicts can be solved by our advanced weapons. Unfortunately, new wars fought with new technologies will not be nearly as easy as the public has been led to believe. Worse yet, those same new technologies that so enthrall us may actually increase the chances of war.

In my 2017 book *Future War: Preparing for the New Global Battlefield*, I described new technologies that would change the nature of warfare and would challenge soldiers to think about the proper ways to employ those technologies on the battlefield. In addition to discussing the moral and ethical implications of the new technologies, *Future War* called upon the public and our political leaders to pay more attention to the dramatic effects that technology would have, and to consider more carefully the employment of a new generation of weapons and the promises made for those weapons.

The reaction to *Future War* was a combination of fear and uncertainty—fear that we are moving too quickly toward high-tech warfare and uncertainty about what to do about it. This reaction was precisely the result for which I had hoped. Reviews of the book were generally positive, with some legitimate criticism that it raised too many questions and provided too few answers. The book generated numerous requests for lectures. My own experience at the University of Notre Dame, where I have taught a highly popular course, "The Ethics of Emerging Weapons Technologies," has been that young people have an unmet need for information on the critical topics of war and peace and are vitally interested in questions of ethics and morality. What was a bit unanticipated was the foreign response to *Future War*. Foreign journalists and foreign military leaders expressed a strong interest. The book was translated into six languages. I can only surmise that, given the technological prowess of the US military and its almost ubiquitous presence around the globe, citizens of other countries harbor interests or concerns about how the US might fight in future conflicts in their parts of the world.

After *Future War*, I realized from the many questions I had received and the debates and discussions in which I had participated that there was not only enormous interest in new weapons technologies and their moral implications but also a real concern that the technologies themselves might contribute to starting a war. The worry here is that we will mistakenly view technological sophistication as a predictor of success. Additionally, while *Future War* dwelt on the just war theory concerns about *jus in bello* (justice in war), there also needed to be discussion of how the new technologies might affect issues of *jus ad bellum* (justice in going to war).

Future Peace: Technology, Aggression, and the Rush to War picks up the thread, adding information and context to many of the issues raised in *Future War*, like our dangerous overreliance on technology, while raising new issues and asking questions about motivations for war and what can be done to resist the multiple and ever-increasing urges for groups and countries to resort to violent conflict. It focuses on one set of technologies, the serious issues of autonomous systems and the application of artificial intelligence to weapons and, more specifically, the command and control systems that govern them. The book describes the globally deployed and thinly stretched military with its high-tech and highly automated, networked systems that are arrayed against similarly equipped competitors in tense situations around the globe.

It depicts the growing animosity between the US and its adversaries and a high-pressure world in which the presence of militaries bristling with old and new weapons, deployed by gunslinger political leaders, and increasingly controlled by software and computers, has the potential to erupt into violence. It describes the many urges to violence, shows how technologies are abetting those urges, and explores what can be done to mitigate not only dangerous human behaviors but dangerous technical behaviors as well. Like *Future War*, *Future Peace* addresses the disgraceful lack of knowledge of the public and some politicians concerning important issues of foreign policy, war, and peace. Worse yet, politicians appear to see the armed forces as just another tool to implement their agendas, lacking any sensitivity to, or consideration of, the human dimensions of armed conflict. Peace is possible, but it will require intensive efforts on the part of technologists, military leaders, diplomats, politicians, and the public. *Future Peace* amplifies some well-known ideas about how to address the issues and provides far-, mid-, and short-term recommendations for actions that will be needed to reverse the apparent headlong rush into conflict. It is not about being totally antiwar or stopping wars altogether. That would be unrealistic. Rather, it is about doing all we can to prevent unnecessary wars and to end those that do occur as soon and as humanely as possible. My overriding concern, and the reason I wrote *Future Peace*, is to draw attention to the fact that we, collectively, are not paying enough attention to the growing influence complex technologies are having on warfare and, critically, the role technology plays in the motivations of our leadership to employ military forces. In the past, even the new technologies for war were relatively simple and their effects more predictable. Today's technologies are rapidly exceeding our ability to understand them, how they operate, or what their long-term consequences might be.

Like the previous work, *Future Peace* raises many questions for which it has insufficient, unsatisfying, or no answers. While it attempts to find solutions to the problems raised, the issues remain exceedingly complex, sometimes perhaps even intractable. There is value, nonetheless, in shining a bright spotlight on the questions and beginning a widespread dialogue about them.

Scholars in previous eras debated whether technology would solve all the ills of society or become an enslaving force. These so-called *crises of modernity* caused writers of the day to take radical positions on whether to deify technology or demonize it as an evil force.[1] Today, as the level of technological complexity in both daily life and issues of war and weapons increases seemingly exponentially, we are faced with a similar crisis. Unfortunately, as technology gets more complex, the willingness of citizens and politicians to try to understand diminishes. Studies conclude that citizens actually do have the capacity to understand science to a level needed to make informed decisions but that such issues often fall below their level of interest.[2] The more difficult the subject, the more likely an individual will simply give up trying—not a good thing under any circumstances, but especially dangerous in the case of war.

My thoughts and the associated public speaking and writing have not always been about ways to avoid or end wars, nor have they always focused on concepts of just war theory and laws of war. Growing up in a family of veterans, in an economically depressed and deeply conservative area, I tended toward an early worldview that was relatively unquestioning and patriotic and was critical of anyone or anything that seemed too liberal, soft on communism, or dismissive of the president or the military. That began to change when I encountered a mild-mannered but deceptively revolutionary and open-minded teacher of literature. Then too, I was stunned by the deaths of several hometown friends in the early phases of combat in Vietnam. While studying physics and engineering in college—along with military tactics in the reserve officer training corps (ROTC)—I also encountered entirely new areas of literature and philosophy and social sciences that opened my eyes and broadened my theretofore narrow worldview. As an army officer during the Vietnam War, I trained diligently for combat, but I began to see more clearly that everything was not actually as clear-cut as I had previously thought. Arguments about avoiding the dreaded "domino effect" of rampant communism in Southeast Asia rang a bit hollow. In the army in Europe during the Cold War, I embraced with great seriousness the need, and was prepared, to confront the Soviet Union with force and ultimately with tactical nuclear weapons if necessary. The experience, however, left me with lingering questions about the sense, or, more accurately, the insanity, of a potentially civilization-ending conflict based on a difference in ideologies. For a lifelong scientist/engineer and technocrat, a subsequent two-and-a-half-decade career in the air force was better than I could ever have anticipated, a technologist's dream, leading me into high-tech research and development in space surveillance and intelligence systems. As I grew more senior, however, I began to recoil at the almost-unthinking embrace of technology and the enormous expenditures on research and weapons development and purchases. The attacks of September 11, 2001, convinced me, along with everyone else, of the need for action to avenge those senseless murders of innocent people and to try to rid the world of such cowardly actors. Unfortunately, the response to 9/11 became, as I have written, far too extreme and soon began to violate basic moral and ethical principles of war and the military profession. Enormous sums of money were thrown at an array of technologies—some worthwhile, some just opportunistic—intended to track down and eliminate terrorists around the globe. A dangerous militarism seemed to characterize our behavior, aided and abetted by technological arrogance and vast resources. We were guilty of "mission myopia," focusing on operational goals and dismissing any concern over what we were doing to accomplish them. Thus began my postretirement involvement with the University of Notre Dame, teaching and writing about war, technology, ethics and the laws of armed conflict, and international humanitarian law, and ultimately to the writing of *Future War*, and now *Future Peace*.

ACKNOWLEDGMENTS

I am exceedingly grateful for the encouragement and active support of many people and organizations in the research and completion of this work. Like war, the subject of peace can be addressed in an almost infinite number of ways. I benefited greatly from the focusing suggestions of many colleagues.

I first want to express my deep appreciation to the University of Notre Dame Institute for Advanced Study (NDIAS) for their generous support and for the opportunity to spend an academic year in residence among a group of such accomplished scholars. My thanks especially go to Brad Gregory, the former NDIAS director, for selecting me, and to current director Meghan Sullivan for her continued strong support. The staff, including Kristian Olsen and Carolyn Sherman, made the research effort efficient and enjoyable, and the resources of the University of Notre Dame Library were simply astounding.

I am deeply indebted to Notre Dame professors Michael Desch, David Cortright, and Daniel Philpott and to University of Wisconsin-Madison professor Claire Wendland for their close reading and suggestions for the manuscript. The diversity of their suggestions, from content to style, dramatically improved the work. I learned much from their writing as well. Notre Dame philosophy professor Don Howard reviewed and commented on the manuscript continuously from its early stages to its completion, and we had many rich discussions about its content. John Balkcom, chair of the Governing Board of the *Bulletin of the Atomic Scientists*, provided extensive and useful feedback. Thanks also go to Notre Dame professors Robert Goulding, Emanuele Ratti, Ian Johnson, Jerry McKenny, Gerald Powers, Atalia Omer, and Craig Iffland for participating in my seminars and providing valuable inputs, and to the other NDIAS Fellows who followed my work throughout the academic year and who made great recommendations for improvement.

No set of acknowledgments would be complete without prominent mention of the extraordinary work of my undergraduate research assistants Maria Keller and Andrew Lischke. More than simply helping to identify and locate sources, Maria closely read each of many iterations of the manuscript and provided helpful recommendations for content and structure, in addition to editing. Her inputs were influential and her suggestions almost always followed. Andrew assisted for one semester and provided several very useful suggestions for research sources.

As always, even while I sought and incorporated inputs from respected colleagues, the work is my own, and I bear full responsibility for its direction and content.

I am deeply indebted to Stephen Wrinn and Rachel Kindler of the University of Notre Dame Press for enthusiastically embracing this work and for including me in their list of superb authors.

This work is dedicated to my wife, Dale, who unhesitatingly supported my work, my pursuit of the NDIAS fellowship, and the move to Notre Dame. She and my children have long provided much of the foundation and underpinnings for my thinking on contemporary issues.

INTRODUCTION

And not one will know of the war, not one
Will care at least when it is done.

Not one would mind, neither bird nor tree
If mankind perished utterly;

And Spring herself, when she woke at dawn,
Would scarcely know that we were gone.
—From Sara Teasdale, "There Will Come Soft Rains"

Sara Teasdale's lyrical poem "There Will Come Soft Rains" at first appears to describe a postapocalyptic, postnuclear world but, written in 1918, was actually a response to the wanton devastation of World War I. At once a paean to the environment and the beauty of the natural world, it was also an indictment of the irrational, destructive nature of humans and the absolute futility of their war making.[1]

It has been just over a century since the end of World War I, a war widely considered to be wholly unnecessary and excessively brutal. The events leading to that war were not rational causes for plunging the globe into total war, and the insanity and mercilessness with which it was fought frightened even the most callous observers. This was a war in which new technologies promised quick victories but had the opposite effect, and in which the massive egos of national leaders prevented meaningful discussions.[2] Indeed, if there was ever a case when war was irrational, this was it. More than nine million soldiers and five million civilians are estimated to have perished under occupation, bombardment, hunger, and disease.[3]

In the twentieth century alone, 108 million people were killed in wars. One researcher boldly estimates that the world has been completely at peace for a mere 268 of the past 3,000 years.[4] Since September 11, 2001, direct war deaths have numbered 480,000, with over 240,000 civilians killed as a result of fighting.[5] This raises the inevitable question, what do we mean by peace? Is it only the absence of armed conflict? This is clearly the major goal, but perhaps it also means that people can live in safety, without fear or threat of violence from any source, including their own government, or that they live in a society where there is a rule of law.

Certainly, the Cold War was largely without armed conflict between the superpowers, but no one would call that a peaceful period. Rebel groups, guerrillas, and terrorists were, and still are, active all around the globe. Some foreign leaders have oppressed, or even killed, their own people and continue to do so. Starvation still plagues parts of sub-Saharan Africa. That doesn't sound like peace.

In the last century, the numbers of war dead have been steadily decreasing. However, while the absolute number of deaths has fallen, the frequency of smaller conflicts has risen and deaths of noncombatants have increased at an alarming rate.[6] While armed conflict is down, the potential for it is dramatically higher now than it has been in recent memory. Harvard psychologist Steven Pinker concludes that since war and combat deaths have continually dropped over time, the world is becoming more peaceful. Viewed from the perspective of classic armed conflict, perhaps, but that is far too narrow a conception to arrive at such a rosy conclusion. Pinker fails to account for the large number of "peacetime" deaths of innocents and noncombatants due to internal strife and repression and sectarian conflicts fought increasingly among the populace. As author John Gray suggests, rather than merely focusing on the fact that war is declining, we should accept that the differences between war and peace are becoming fatally blurred.[7]

Unsurprisingly, many, if not most, of the current conflicts have their roots in long-standing ethnic and political rivalries. Superpowers avoid directly confronting one another for fear of escalation into nuclear conflict, but the list of proxy wars is long. It includes the Korean War, the Soviet invasions of Hungary, Czechoslovakia, and Afghanistan, the Vietnam War, military aid to insurgents in Syria, and the proxy war between the US and Russia that is being waged in Ukraine, to name only a few. Now, advanced technologies are available to more participants. They make war easier and are making matters worse.

War has been a central feature of human societies for millennia. Its character has changed dramatically over time with the growth in populations and the inexorable advance in weaponry. Numerous economic and sociological studies have found a surprising regularity and cyclical nature of war and conflict and have even attempted to correlate upswings in technological innovation with the frequency of outbreaks of violence.[8] So-called modern war marked a sharp increase in destructiveness. The Napoleonic Wars following the French Revolution fundamentally transformed armed conflict.[9] Wars became larger in scale and more totally destructive. The Industrial Revolution accelerated this trend, introducing numerous new technologies that contributed to the slaughter of World War I. Since then, of course, technology has raced even further, with an awful increase in destructive power.

The latter decades of the nineteenth century and the years leading up to World War I reflected an increasing industrialization of warfare, with weapons becoming ever more deadly and with the increasing mechanization and dehumanization of combat. The Crimean War (1853–56) and the US Civil War (1861–65) marked the emergence of a large and powerful armaments industry and the beginning of a widespread dependence on advanced technologies and weapons.[10] The rapid growth in weapons arsenals suggested a potential to use those weapons. Countries engage in arms races to achieve qualitative and numerical superiority. War is more likely when the offense has an advantage, and as classic "offense-defense theory" predicts, that likelihood is shaped by the technology that is available.[11] American culture, enamored as it is with technology, is prone to technological hubris and holds a fundamental belief that any adversary can be defeated by our technological and material superiority.[12] Such hubris has undoubtedly led decision makers to resort to conflict rather than do the hard work of diplomacy. One need look no further than the 2003 US invasion of Iraq, which was supposed to make quick work of a technologically inferior enemy. Technology for war has advanced at dizzying speed with the development of the airplane and the tank in World War I, radar and nuclear weapons in World War II, later the development of precision-guided bombs, and now computer and information-based weapons.

The character of conflict is now changing yet again and in seemingly arbitrary ways. The United States has been involved in some type of armed conflict for almost two decades, but sometimes it is unclear why, and who the enemy actually is. Much of that time has been spent waging a nebulous "war on terror." And our engagements have not been so-called classic wars. There are new tactics, including crime, guerrilla activities, and other mischief, in what is often referred to as "hybrid war" or war in the "gray zone." The 2014 Russian incursion and annexation of Crimea stands as a perfect example, with its "little green men"—soldiers whose uniforms bore no identifying markings.[13] Today's wars are unlike the more predictable affairs of the past: the techniques and tools adapt themselves to the environment within which they are fought.[14] While we are not at war, per se, the world is certainly not at peace. It could also be argued that we are again in a new "Cold War," with China now being added to the standoff with the US. There are no armed conflicts among superpowers, but the relations are antagonistic and the actions increasingly provocative.

Militaries, especially the US, are heavily dependent on computer-controlled and soon to be autonomous systems for everything from logistics, to command and control, to actual killing. Increasingly, decisions are being taken out of the hands of human beings. At the same time, the major powers and others are becoming more bellicose and aggressive. The worry is that these trends—automation and aggressiveness—like the superposition of waves, will interact and amplify one another, exacerbating an already dangerous, high-pressure national security situation around the globe.

The US military is heavily armed, deployed all over the world, and connected and controlled by a vast computer and communications network. The highly networked nature of military forces worldwide and their heavily armed status present us with the possibility of a "hair-trigger" situation and mentality. There are ways we can technically modulate military behavior and responses, however, and the public can and should demand more accountability from its leaders concerning the control and use of its military.

Technologies for war are developing rapidly and are becoming more available to nations besides the so-called superpowers. Instant communications are causing events to unfold with frightening speed and with sometimes unfiltered and erroneous information. In earlier eras there was a time lag between an event and a potential response. Now everything is connected to everything else, and any action demands an instant reaction. These trends, in tandem with the confusion that springs from a growing vulnerability of data and information, do not bode well for a peaceful world. It is urgent that they be addressed, mitigated, and, hopefully, reversed.

The time scales of warfare have shrunk dramatically. The ubiquity of networks, rapid global communications, and computer-aided decision-making, the twenty-four-hour news cycle, and the omnipresence of social media have all conspired to minimize the ability of a military commander to take the time necessary to properly assess a situation, think through rational courses of action, and decide. In 1807, after the British attack on the USS *Chesapeake*, it took four months and a round-trip ocean crossing for communications between President Jefferson and British foreign secretary George Canning to decide the US response.[15] That time allowed the situation to be defused and the outrage of the population to abate. In the Civil War, we had the telegraph. In World War I we had radio. Today we have satellite communications. Whereas before there was time to consider, debate, and reflect, the current drive toward the use of automated and autonomous decision-making seems to push things even further toward an authoritarian, literally nonhuman way of identifying and responding to threats. Time has become a tyrant to be deposed as a controlling factor in our decision-making. However, the systems we use are designed and built by humans, and those same humans can ensure that the systems operate in a way that preserves peace rather than inciting war. It is only for us to demand it.

The unfortunate fact is that the major world powers—and many emerging ones—are excessively militaristic. The US in particular tends to view global issues as requiring military responses. We see this in the growth of the defense budget and the dramatic cuts to the State Department and the diplomatic corps. Defense budgets worldwide are growing, and countries are deploying their militaries around the world with more frequency. Diplomacy is taking a back seat to militarism. Spending on new weapons technologies in particular is growing rapidly. These technologies will add new capabilities to an already-large arsenal of lethal weapons possessed by nations around the world. Something must be done to ensure that the new weapons and systems are properly controlled and that militaries around the world find ways to reduce the chances of war, not increase them.

Countries and groups around the world are heavily armed, and the global arms industries provide a steady flow of weapons for their use. There are flashpoints everywhere—Russia and eastern Europe, China and the South China Sea, the Middle East, the Korean Peninsula, and Africa, to name a few. There are numerous issues—both diplomatic and technical—driving the competition, and there are any number of ways in which we might get drawn into conflict in those areas. In each case, the availability of advanced technologies and weapons is a prime motivator of, or at least an excuse for, behavior.

The ready availability and large stocks of advanced weapons provide the implements of war, but festering problems among the world's populations set the conditions for violent conflict. Income disparity, religious and ethnic hatred, lack of education, arms proliferation, demand for respect by other countries, instant availability of information, and the promise of new superweapons are some of the forces pushing countries and groups toward violence.

Today, technology almost always plays a role in either causing the violence or contributing to it. Hezbollah employs rockets to terrorize Israel. Israel destroyed a Syrian nuclear facility using a combination of cyber and electronic warfare techniques and kinetic weapons.[16] The

2003 Iraq War was fought, ostensibly, to prevent that country from deploying weapons of mass destruction. In 2008, Russia employed cyberattacks in its invasion of Georgia, and unmanned aerial vehicles were used in that conflict. In 2015, Russian cyber forces shut down the Ukrainian power grid. These developments further confuse classic, long-held views of warfare.

War is ethically and morally problematic. Over the centuries and decades, after the introduction of new styles of conflict and new weapons, nations have seen fit to place restrictions on their armies. With time, a set of rules and standards emerged to limit the brutality and curb the excesses of combatants. Norms of behavior were established to protect the innocent, and the use of inhumane weapons was outlawed. International laws, like the Geneva Conventions and the prohibitions on chemical and biological weapons, have resulted. In light of the long-standing proclivities to war and the emergence of a new class of technologies for fighting wars, it is imperative that we step back and consider again the moral and ethical implications of weapons employing these technologies and wars employing these weapons.

The tenets of just war theory and the laws of armed conflict are dependent on the decisions of human beings. This is important. Topics of *jus ad bellum* (justice in going to war) require decisions about proper authority, right intention, just cause, last resort, and others that are just not in the purview of a machine. The idea of a machine having intentions or making judgments about justice is simply meaningless. Likewise, requirements of *jus in bello* (justice in war) cannot be decided by a machine. Decisions about military necessity, proportionality, legitimate combatants, and what constitutes unnecessary and superfluous suffering raise deep questions of fairness, human dignity, and morality and are the province of human commanders. The original just war concepts were developed in a time when limitations on war making were constrained by the weapons themselves. The evolution to so-called modern war, and today's hyperwar, in which technology has rendered those constraints obsolete, makes the search for restraint ever more critical.

The American public is dangerously uninvolved, and seemingly uninterested in, questions of the use of the military around the globe. Admittedly, there are sometimes good and valid reasons for military force, but data on deployments show that US armed forces have been repeatedly used by presidents, often with questionable rationale. Why is the public not more critical? We must find ways to involve the citizens in issues of war and use of military forces and to identify ways of slowing the rapid resort to arms, raising barriers to political leaders who more often than not take the military route in lieu of doing the hard work of diplomacy. We must slow down the impulses to action and push back against them.

Throughout history, statesmen, military leaders, religious leaders, and intellectuals have decried violence and argued against war. Strong, respected voices of reason spoke up through the media of the day and often resisted the calls for war. Today, few, if any, such voices exist, and even when they do, they are drowned out by others in the press, on the internet, and on social media. Thought leaders will have to adapt more quickly to this reality if they are to once again regain credibility. Voices of restraint must provide a rationale against military conflict and highlight the damage, unseen by the public, that it does to the country.

But we cannot just rely on people. Changes to rectify this dangerous state of affairs must be both structural and technical. Resistors and capacitors are important elements in damping the sometimes wild and uncontrolled oscillations of electrical circuits and other physical systems. We must find a conceptual way of building such damping devices into the complex computer and communication networks of the military command and control system, as well as the upper levels of decision-making, to tamp down the urge to action. We must deploy some speed brakes, both physical and human, into the system to resist the urges to violence and the propensity to act in the absence of rational thought.

The military is a vast, widely deployed, overstressed enterprise with highly complex systems. The world is a pressure cooker. There are numerous places and opportunities for the system to be thrown out of equilibrium, and our command and control system must be up to the task of preventing such an occurrence. Added to the situation is the fact that far too many urges to violence push us toward war and away from peace. We must find ways to reduce the pressure, limit knee-jerk reactions, and resist the urges to war.

ONE

———————●———————

A GIANT ARMED NERVOUS SYSTEM

A strange game. The only winning move is not to play.
—War Games, 1983

———————————————

In the early morning of September 26, 1983, Lieutenant Colonel Stanislav Petrov of the Soviet Air Defense Forces was on duty in the Moscow command center where the Soviet military monitored its early-warning satellites over the United States. Suddenly and unexpectedly the alarms went off, warning that nuclear-armed intercontinental ballistic missiles had been launched from an American base. Colonel Petrov was obliged to report the incident

9

to his superiors at the warning-system headquarters and ultimately to the Soviet leadership, who would decide whether or not to launch a retaliatory attack.

All of his computer-controlled electronic systems were warning him of imminent nuclear destruction, but with years of personal experience under his belt, Colonel Petrov struggled to absorb and make sense of streams of incoming information, ultimately deciding to ignore the alarms because the launch reports were probably false. He later explained that it was a gut decision, based on his distrust of the early-warning system and the small amount of credible data.

But for the sane, reasoned approach and calm nerves of one skeptical—human—individual, the advanced technologies of the military systems of the time might have plunged the world into a doomsday thermonuclear war.

THE MILITARY: A VAST, FAR-FLUNG ENTERPRISE

The US military is huge, deployed all over the world, highly interconnected and increasingly automated, and heavily armed. With large investments in high-speed and high-bandwidth communications, and connecting its weapons in a vast internet-of-things, the military is becoming, as one commentator says, "a giant armed nervous system"—an interesting and apt description.[1]

There are approximately 1.3 million men and women on active duty, of whom 200,000 are stationed overseas in 143 countries. There are 750,000 Department of Defense civilians and 1.1 million National Guard and reserve personnel.[2] The individual military services train, organize, and equip forces that they then provide to combatant commanders to carry out specific missions as ordered by the national command authorities.

Armed forces of major military powers are deployed around the globe. In excess of 60,000 US forces are stationed in Germany and other western European countries, and deployed forward in Poland, Romania, and Hungary. In Asia, there are over 130,000 American troops, largely in Japan, Hawaii, and South Korea. The air force has strategic bombers in Okinawa. The navy has aircraft carrier battle groups steaming in the South China Sea. Around the world, there are US special operations troops in over a hundred different countries. Russia has large numbers of troops and equipment in Syria, Armenia, Moldova, Georgia, Ukraine, and Belarus. China has forces in Hong Kong and on the mainland, directly across the straits from Taiwan.

US combat forces are organized into regional commands and functional commands, each headed by a four-star officer. There are regional combatant commanders for the Indo-Pacific region, Europe, the Middle East, Africa, Latin America, and the US homeland. There are functional combatant commands for transportation, special operations, nuclear, space, and cyber missions. There are forces in over eight hundred bases around the world, many in inhospitable areas where troops operate under dangerous conditions.[3] Of the deployed troops, the largest concentrations are in Asia (38 percent), Europe (32 percent), and the Middle East and Africa (13 percent).[4] There are thousands of aircraft, hundreds of ships, including aircraft carriers and submarines, and tens of thousands of combat vehicles. Nine countries have their own nuclear weapons, with five others hosting them for the US. While other countries have military forces deployed, none, by far, has such a worldwide presence as the US.

Connectivity between military units and with command elements is essential with such widely dispersed units. Deployed forces depend heavily on a concept called "reach-back," in which they are dependent on assured communications and logistics with headquarters in the US and central locations in Europe or Asia. The military is almost totally dependent on networks for both tactical and strategic command and control, logistics, services, communications, and even weapons functions. Those networks depend on thousands of miles of high-speed optical fiber cables under the ocean and scores of communications satellites orbiting the earth. War is increasingly conducted using networks of computers, weapons, sensors, and electronic warfare systems. The heavy dependence on these networks poses serious challenges, particularly if combat results in interrupted connectivity, limited data rates, or disruption as a result of electronic or physical attack. The ever-increasing sophistication and global nature of those networks make the information environment more extensive, more complicated, and more complex than ever before.

Accurate data and information are essential to military planners and commanders of combat units. The US has a vast array of sensors around the globe. There are sensors on most aircraft, ships, and vehicles. There are also space-based sensors. Satellites monitor the earth for missile launches and are used for photoreconnaissance and signal detection. They provide accurate position, navigation, and timing signals for everything from financial systems, to personal automobiles, to missiles and bombs. Ground radars and telescopes, as well as on-orbit systems, keep track of objects in space and on the ground. All of these sensors feed the battle management systems that will be employed in the event of a conflict.

Military forces use multiple networks, the sensitivity of which depends on the sensitivity of the data and missions being performed. There are commercial networks, an unclassified military-only network, a secret-level network known as SIRP (secret internet router protocol), and the JWICS (joint worldwide intelligence communications system) for top-secret data. Much in the way of effort and resources goes into keeping these systems secure. The DOD has the world's biggest network of networks, with a budget of close to $40 billion, about ten thousand operational systems, hundreds of data centers, tens of thousands of servers, millions of computers and devices, and hundreds of thousands of commercial mobile devices.[5] Add to that a heavy dependence on both commercial and dedicated military satellites, microwave, and optical fiber networks. DOD supports more than forty agencies and manages about four million cyber identity credentials.

In today's scenarios, speed is—more than ever—of the essence. Military commanders have limited time to obtain an accurate assessment of the situation, to assess potential courses of action, and to make decisions. They operate under extreme time pressures and high operational tempo. Furthermore, they need to draw from all possible sources to ensure that the most complete and relevant picture can be created of the situation, in near real time, and to understand the implications of their decisions and courses of action—a tall order under the best of circumstances. Such time pressures will inevitably lead commanders to depend more heavily on automated and autonomous systems. Despite our best intentions and our protestations to the contrary, technology is forcing us to depend on it and is chipping away at the idea of *meaningful* human control.

Army leaders are demanding high-speed, mobile, secure command and control systems, allowing them to move rapidly in the midst of a violent fight, all the while staying connected.[6] Communicating in garrison is one thing, communicating on the move is quite another. It requires secure satellite and jam-resistant communications and a lot of bandwidth. A former chief of naval operations wants to "network everything to everything,"[7] and the air force chief of staff goes even further, saying that victory in future combat will depend less on individual capabilities and more on a fully networked force.[8]

Describing a vision of future warfare and the systems needed to practice it, one technical report has discussed the current approach as a need for an "information superiority-enabled concept of operations that generates increased combat power by networking sensors, decision-makers, and shooters, increasing the speed of command and higher tempo of operations"[9]—in other words, doing the same things they have always done, only faster. The worry here is that this overwhelming concern with speed ignores the complexity, uncertainty, and chaos of the future and perhaps current battlefield, and that it may blind commanders to other, more nuanced information—context, for instance. The hyperconnectedness of military forces and the possibility of AI-mediated command and control systems means that decision-making can occur at speeds vastly superior to the traditional means of waging war. War will be fast. It will be *hyperwar*.[10]

One of the problems with such speedy decisions, however, is that they may crowd out the opportunity for diplomatic efforts or negotiations and may lead directly to a military solution. Given the historical proclivity of US political leaders to opt for military action and their preference for technology solutions, such pressure may tip the balance. Fast decisions, however, may not always be the best in a crisis.[11] We may be faster, but it will be *speed at the expense of understanding*. With such great degrees of automation and such demands for speed, our decisions may evolve from being well considered to being merely pro forma. Military planners and leaders may, in fact, be operating under the delusion of control.

In recent years, there has been a fundamental change in weapons and technology employed and considered for use by militaries around the world. To be sure, countries continue to arm themselves with aircraft, ships, tanks, artillery, and other classic weapons. Missile technologies of all types are proliferating rapidly, to include a growing interest in super-high-speed, or hypersonic, missiles. In the end, the military will ultimately resort to kinetic means to destroy an enemy, but computers and information technologies are critical even to what used to be such "simple" weapons. Those classic weapons, too, have become far more complex and sophisticated, highly instrumented with sensors, networked together, and more accurate and lethal. Now, new technologies, such as drones and robots, lasers, cyber warfare, electronic warfare, hypersonics, neuroscience, and even new forms of biological warfare, are being developed. The military is preparing for war in every domain of combat to include space and cyberspace as well as the classic air, sea, and ground domains. The 2020 defense budget, for example, includes $14 billion for space, $10 billion for cyber, $4.6 billion for AI and autonomy, and $2.6 billion for hypersonic weapons.[12]

As if figuring out how to use and control the new technologies individually weren't confusing enough, numerous researchers have begun to address the challenges of technology convergence in which many of the technologies are combined in an interdisciplinary way. Examples include human performance research that includes elements of biotechnology, nanotechnology, information technology, and neuroscience. High-speed weapons like hypersonic missiles and lasers, combined with artificial intelligence and autonomy in command and control, challenge the technical capabilities of most decision makers to understand. A central feature of a future war will be the speed with which it will be conducted. War will just be too fast for a human to keep up. The loss of valuable decision time, increasing technological complexity, insufficient training, and the inability to understand the implications of these developments conspire against reasoned judgments.

Doing the same thing they've always done, only faster, requires commanders to have the latest in information technologies. This class of technologies includes such computer-related topics as artificial intelligence, autonomy, target recognition, microelectronics, and the internet-of-things. Hypersonic weapons, cyber warfare, electronic warfare, and directed-energy weapons will all have a need for machine-based command and control. While human conflict will likely always end in traditional forms of violence, for now, as one writer said, "The digital age has given rise to a connectivity-enabled form of cognitive warfare."[13] A senior Chinese People's Liberation Army officer has written that "the human brain will become a new combat space" and that "success on the future battlefield will require achieving mental/cognitive dominance."[14] We will have to not only outfight our adversaries but also outthink them.

Technologies that will influence the future of war include machine-to-machine communication, augmented reality, and predictive technologies like data mining and machine learning. And, at the moment, artificial intelligence looms large in the pantheon of advanced technologies. All of these technologies will operate amid the *internet-of-things,* a concept that involves the pervasive presence of an enormous number of smart things, things with embedded sensors, in the environment. By means of both wireless and wired connections, they are able to interact to reach common goals. They can behave intelligently and share information with other objects. The commercial internet-of-things is expected to top fifty billion devices by 2025. The military version has grown accordingly. Like the civilian world, the military is instrumenting everything with sensors in an internet-of-battlefield-things. The individual soldier acts as a sensor, sending data back to headquarters; weapon systems have cameras and sensors to detect electronic signals and characterize their environment; satellites collect enormous amounts of data—all networked; and the vast military supply system could not operate without the use of the internet, RFID (radio-frequency identification) tags, and other computer tracking devices. Virtual reality and augmented reality systems are in development that will allow soldiers to combine real data with sophisticated computer simulations of the combat zone, all presented on a helmet-mounted display. Big data and data-mining technologies are of paramount importance in both civilian and military applications. These technologies can discern patterns and suggest inferences that humans, unable to digest such large volumes of data, never could. With so much data and so many things demanding attention, it may be impossible for humans to attain a true understanding of the situation and its context.

By 2050, two-thirds of the world's population will be in what are being called megacities.[15] Future wars are likely to be fought in these dense urban areas. As if things were not complex enough, states and telecommunications companies around the world are rushing to implement the new 5G communications technologies. The 5G networks are digital cellular networks in which the service areas covered are divided into small geographical cells. They employ higher radio frequencies and differ from current technologies and capabilities in that they carry much higher rates of information but at much shorter distances. Cities are being intensively instrumented, for commercial reasons, with sensors and communications systems, and the advent of this new generation of information technologies will create unbelievable amounts of data. These technologies will vastly increase capacity, reduce data latency by a factor of over a hundred, and increase by many orders of magnitude the numbers of devices transmitting signals—creating a nightmarish electromagnetic environment. While they will enhance communications and commerce, these developments will complicate terribly the situation of forces trying to sort out signals in an already chaotic urban combat situation. Combat in urban areas will be difficult, deadly, indiscriminate, and heavily controlled by technology.

The jamming, deception, and counterelectronic capabilities that the US military will encounter are also becoming much more sophisticated, especially in an era of superfast computing and artificial intelligence. To make matters worse, data, the lifeblood of artificial intelligence, are rarely clean and well structured, nor are they always accurate or unbiased. This will be especially true in combat, where the situation and the context change with frightening speed and the command and control of forces are paramount.

THE IMPORTANCE OF COMMAND AND CONTROL

Like a human, whose central nervous system decides on the actions of, and controls, the organs and peripheral limbs, the military has a command and control (C2) system. The military has been automating its command and control as long as it has been possible to do so. From signaling mirrors in the 1800s, to the semaphore, to the introduction of the radio in the early 1900s, technical ways of communicating quickly and over long distances have been a hallmark of military command and control. The introduction of computers was an enormous advance. Beginning in the 1950s, the military began to automate its systems, and that has continued ever since.[16] As relevant today as it was when it was written, a two-decade-old report by the National Academy of Sciences concluded that the rapid progress in information and communications technologies is a critical success factor in military affairs. These enable the "nervous system" of the military—its command and control systems—to more effectively use the "muscle," its weapons, platforms, and troops.[17] Command and control includes situational awareness and mission management. The term is defined as the exercise of authority and direction by a properly designated commander over assigned and attached forces in the accomplishment of the mission. It is the means by which a commander recognizes what needs to be done and sees to it that appropriate actions are taken. It is a complex interaction of people, procedures, and equipment. It is at once a process and also a grouping of computer and communications systems to carry out that process.

Military command and control is often described in terms of *centralized control, decentralized execution*, much as we think about the human central nervous system. The implication is, of course, that the central authority decides and is always in control and that the distributed units (or, in the case of humans, the peripheral nervous system and appendages) faithfully execute their orders. However, the military system—especially now with the advent of AI in command and control—also resembles in many ways the nervous system of an octopus.

THE FASCINATING OCTOPUS

The octopus brain has a large number of neurons—roughly half a billion—in relation to its body size. It is not surprising, then, that the creature can exhibit complex behaviors.[18] Research into cephalopod behavior suggests that the arms of the octopuses may have "minds" of their own. Studies have shown that each individual arm has an independent nervous system and that the centralized brain serves simply to delegate orders, though the arm itself is responsible for deciding exactly how the order will be carried out. Two-thirds of the estimated five hundred million neurons of the octopus are distributed throughout the arms, each of which is controlled by its own ganglion, leading some researchers to a *distributed brain* hypothesis. In one study, researchers severed the nerves in the arms of octopuses, disconnecting them from the rest of the body and brain. The researchers would then tickle the arm of the octopus, which elicited a response as though the nerves were not severed.[19] Essentially, the brain is able to give a quick assignment to the arm and then is no longer required to think about it, allowing the arm's nervous system to take over. The octopus's arms have a neural ring, much like a local area network, that bypasses the brain, so the arms can send information to each other without the brain being aware of it. The researchers found that when the octopus's arms acquire information from their environment, the neurons in the arm can process it and initiate action. The brain doesn't have to do a thing.[20] Professor Frank W. Grasso, using somewhat specialized terminology, says of the octopus arms, "The ganglionic [neural] network operates rather like a distributed control network. It may not match the neuroanatomical definition of a brain, but the diversity of behaviors demonstrated by 'decerebrate' octopuses indicates that we are not far off from the truth if we were to conceptualize it as one."[21] Peter Godfrey-Smith likens the octopus's nervous system to a conductor and a group of jazz players. The conductor gives only rough general instructions and trusts the players to play something that works.[22]

Scientists actively advise the military about ways of replicating this capability for troop and command structures. Military forces are trained to be able to operate on their own when cut off from their unit or other outside support, and the parallels between the octopus's "ganglionic neural network" and distributed military operations are striking. Think of the forward-deployed military unit cut off from its headquarters, or the special operations force necessarily operating autonomously in a foreign country. Like the octopus's brain, headquarters gives the assignment. Like the arms of the octopus, the detached units have an array of sensors to determine their environment. Like the octopus's arms, they have information provided to them before loss of communication and the ability, albeit diminished, to calculate appropriate courses of action. And, like the octopus's arms, military units can coordinate with one another with no involvement of headquarters to accomplish the mission.

The gigantic octopus hovers a few feet above the ocean floor, its huge eyes constantly surveying the world around it, its arms splayed out into the murky waters. From one angle it looks one color, from another a different one altogether. Each arm, bristling with numerous suckers and thousands of sensors, looks different. As one of the arms senses motion nearby and determines it is a food source, it reaches out, lightning-like, and captures the unfortunate creature—as the rest of the octopus's thirty-foot, five-hundred-pound bulk remains perfectly still, focused on an approaching threat. The entire mass seems to disappear, taking on the color of the ocean floor, then she is gone in an instant, leaving behind a swirling inky screen to cover her departure.

The octopus is a predator. It is also sneaky. It has a unique ability to change both its shape and its coloration in response to a threat and to engage in deception and camouflage to confuse its enemies. The octopus is an opportunistic explorer, curious, ingenious, and adaptable in its behavior.[23] It has long evoked fascination. Even ancient writers commented on its unusual cleverness.[24] It has been described as mischievous, playful, and devious, with uncanny intelligence. Military scientists are now studying how to recreate some octopus capabilities and model their behavior for military denial and deception. There is something about this fascinating creature that is both awe-inspiring and enigmatic, characteristics to which military forces aspire.

MILITARY COMMAND AND CONTROL SYSTEMS

One of the primary elements of the command and control systems used by all forces is the Global Command and Control System (GCCS), which includes various data-processing and Web services used to support combat operations, troop movements, intelligence analysis, targeting, and analysis of radar, terrain, and weather. These systems do everything from figuring out how much fuel combat aircraft will need and when they have to refuel, how many of what kinds of armaments they should carry, and when reinforcements may be needed, to relaying the commander's actual orders. They identify threats, help develop courses of action, analyze risks, and present a hugely important common operational picture showing location and disposition of enemy and friendly forces. Systems such as GCCS ingest and use data from hundreds of different sources. The military often refers to its systems as "battle management, command and control systems" to include the functions of actual control of weapons during conflict.

Command and control systems reside largely in operations centers, both deployed and in the US. There are, of course, the well-known ones like White House Situation Room and the National Military Command Center at the Pentagon. The US Space Force has its Combined Space Operations Center. The National Security Agency and US Cyber Command have the Joint Operations Center and the Integrated Cyber Center. In the field, the air force has its Air Operations Centers (AOCs), the army has its Tactical Operations Centers (TOCs), and the navy has its Combat Information Centers (CICs) aboard ships.

An operations center is a focus of activity, operating around the clock with a constant flow of information and orders. In each case, there are hundreds of electronic feeds of information providing real-time or near-real-time data on threats, intelligence, weapons status, and space information, for example. It is in these centers that command and control systems play a critical role. From these locations, which act like the octopus's brain, commanders will direct units operating on the battlefield.

At a remote outpost in the mountains of Afghanistan sits a large army tent surrounded by barbed wire and guarded by heavily armed soldiers. Inside the perimeter wire are power generators and several communications dishes pointed at military satellites orbiting the earth. The compound bristles with all sorts of radio anten-

nae. Inside, portable air conditioners cool the computers. Bundles of wires crisscross the hastily laid wooden floor. At makeshift desks sit soldiers, a collection of intelligence specialists, space operations experts, logisticians, aircraft planners, and operations specialists. This is the unit command and control center.

Another example of such a center is the US Space Command and North American Aerospace Defense Command (NORAD) Cheyenne Mountain Operations Center (CMOC) in Colorado Springs, Colorado.

In the late 1990s, I commanded the Cheyenne Mountain Operations Center. Buried deep under a mountain and protected by huge blast doors, the CMOC was the central hub of information for strategic warning of an attack on North America. Subcenters devoted to space, air, and missile surveillance reported information from a worldwide array of sensors. Numerous sources of information, including raw data and finished intelligence, flowed uninterrupted through a massive communications hub. Our role was to ensure that the National Command Authorities were notified of a potential attack in a very short time and, ultimately to be able to recommend a national response. Day-to-day operations in the command center were routine and—happily—boring. As in most command centers, however, working there could be characterized by long periods of monotony punctuated by short periods of sheer terror. On countless occasions, satellites would detect the launch of a missile somewhere in the world, and each time, even with the near certainty that the launch was a routine one, the adrenaline level in the center would rise until we could figure out what it was. As previous errors had shown, the wrong conclusions about what was happening could take us to the brink of war. Accurate and timely information was essential. Mistakes really were not an option.

While the general concepts of command and control are fundamental, it is important to distinguish the practical differences between nuclear and non-nuclear command and control. Not surprisingly, command and control of nuclear weapons is a special case in which the procedures and systems are subject to intense scrutiny and error checking far beyond that required for non-nuclear systems. As you would expect, the systems and processes designed to prevent errors concerning nuclear war would be extremely strong and error inhibiting. There are rigid rules about everything that goes into nuclear weapons, about who can get anywhere near them, and about how they are moved, maintained, and deployed. Hardware and software are rigorously checked and double-checked before inclusion in a system. Such is the importance of nuclear surety that in 2008 the secretary of defense, Robert Gates, fired the secretary and chief of staff of the US Air Force over lapses in control of weapons and procedures. But the question remains, how strong are these actions for other, non-nuclear, command and control systems?

Nuclear war may not hang in the balance, but tactical operations centers are also critically important. In addition to possibly getting soldiers killed, mistakes at the tactical level can spin out of control and escalate into larger, more general conflicts.

In the mountains of Afghanistan, several of the key personnel in the US Marine Corps unit's command center were recent replacements for soldiers redeployed or killed or wounded in the previous week's battles. The watch officer was new and inexperienced. Soon after the start of the shift, a scout team was sent out to conduct reconnaissance and came under heavy fire from insurgents hiding in the hills. The team sent urgent requests to the command center for help, but the watch officer and command center personnel were unsure of themselves and too slow to react. When they finally dispatched helicopter gunships and a medical team to the area, the deployed unit had sustained heavy casualties, with over half its personnel killed or wounded.

Expertise and experience, familiarity with the mission and the systems, and human leadership are crucial in command and control.[25]

These things simply cannot be automated and expected to work in the chaotic and unpredictable battlefield.

ARTIFICIAL INTELLIGENCE AND AUTONOMOUS SYSTEMS

Conversation [edited] between Dave Bowman, astronaut in Stanley Kubrick's movie 2001: A Space Odyssey, *and HAL, an onboard, artificially intelligent computer.*[26] *HAL has locked Dave outside the space station to prevent him from aborting the mission.*

> DAVE: *Open the pod bay doors, HAL.*
> HAL: *I'm sorry, Dave. I'm afraid I can't do that.*
> DAVE: *What's the problem?*
> HAL: *This mission is too important for me to allow you to jeopardize it.*
> HAL: *I know that you were planning to disconnect me— I cannot allow* [that] *to happen.*
> DAVE: *HAL, I won't argue with you anymore! Open the doors!*
> HAL: *Dave, this conversation can serve no purpose anymore. Goodbye.*

Much has been written about the dangers of advanced intelligences that will take over the world from humans and about the rise of so-called killer robots in military uses. I have spoken and written frequently about the importance of meaningful human control in employing these weapons. However, the almost-singular focus on autonomous killing machines obscures an equally, if not more, important issue. Perhaps because it is an amorphous, distributed problem, and there are no sexy, scary weapons involved, we overlook the fact that the military command and control (C2) system is increasingly and heavily controlled by computers and artificial intelligence.

HAL, the artificially intelligent mastermind of Kubrick's movie, programmed as it was to ensure the completion of its mission and its own survival, took actions that ignored the interests and safety of everyone else. In the real-life scenario at the beginning of this chapter, the thoughtful human, Colonel Petrov, acted against his own near-term interests (opening himself up to a possible court-martial for disobeying orders) and chose to override the answers provided by his sensors and computers, possibly saving the world from destruction. We have no way of knowing if a machine would be capable of such a nuanced decision. There is no prior experience, and thermonuclear war would not be an ideal test case for finding out.

Interest in the technology of artificial intelligence has reached a fever pitch in recent years. Around the world, nations are racing to attain the lead in AI for commercial and financial competition, but for military dominance as well. All of the military services have plans to incorporate AI into both administrative and logistics systems, and into command and control systems at every level in the chain of command. Logistics and supply-chain applications of AI have proven to be of great value in the private sector in increasing efficiency and reducing waste. Military leaders eagerly await developments in command and control systems and anticipate that AI will affect decision-making, although they are unsure exactly how. In the near term, AI will present analysis and recommendations to the commander. Since it will certainly be faster than humans, at some point AI may become better at decision-making than the commanders, and more responsibilities will be delegated to it, eventually possibly replacing some human experts.[27] The danger is not that it won't work or even that it will work too well. The danger is that military planners will assume it works correctly and will trust it to give correct answers. Trust—perhaps misplaced trust—will be the main issue.

Scientists repeatedly make the point that to be truly successful, AI systems must interact with social systems, that is, humans. Philosophers refer to our current world as a "techno-social," one in which our technologies and our social interactions cannot be separated, where technology is embedded and coevolves with social practices, values, and institutions.[28] In turn, scientists say that creativity and innovation are deeply social processes, not capable of being duplicated by a machine. Regarding the holy grail of artificial general intelligence (AGI), they conclude that autonomous software and biologically constructed machines will not be sufficient to generate machine intelligence, saying, "In ways we still do not understand, our social communities and interactions in language are essential for general intelligence."[29] Indeed, what is war but social interaction on a massive and violent scale?

The US Army is working to incorporate AI into every aspect of the future battlefield, including sensors, munitions, autonomous robots, and virtual agents to control networks and wage cyber war.[30] Human/machine integration will improve situational understanding. Machine learning and greater processing power will allow for the generation and critiquing of hypotheses, potential courses of action, and outcomes. First adopters of this emerging technology for decision support will achieve a significant advantage over adversaries.

The army, it appears, is going all in on this technology. However, it may be going too far. A November 2018 symposium of the Association of the US Army Institute of Land Warfare was all about autonomy and artificial intelligence, with panels on such topics as "Autonomy and Artificial Intelligence Enabled Mission Command in Multi-domain Operations." In future wars, humans will be only one of the species of intelligence, sharing all aspects of combat and decision-making with machines.[31] The future battlefield has been described as one where AI will be ubiquitous. It will be in everything from weapons, to support equipment, to command and control. Every soldier will be a sensor, and weapons will autonomously sense the situation, decide, and ultimately act.[32] If that sounds somewhat improbable, consider what the Defense Advanced Research Projects Agency (DARPA) is trying to achieve. They are working on a project that, if successful, would, teach an AI system operating in the midst of combat to learn and react appropriately without needing to be retrained. The program would, in DARPA's words, "empower machines to go through the standard military process themselves—observe the situation, orient to what they observe, decide the best course of action, *and then act*."[33] A former vice-chairman of the Joint Chiefs of Staff recently told a seminar of strategists to get used to the fact that lethal AI is real, saying, "We're going to have to figure out how to do it and feel like we're controlling it."[34]

There is an ever-increasing trend to turn decision-making over to machines. One study found that as of 2016 some form of AI was in 284 weapon systems worldwide.[35] That decline of human decision-making is worrisome. In the past, accomplished military leaders personally controlled the tempo and guided the battle. Human beings are capable of empathetic and good, sometimes counterintuitive, decisions. Machines, even very smart ones, are unlikely to be capable of such nuance in armed conflict, an area of human activity where it is needed most.

Imagine a situation in a hostile location overseas. A seasoned, battle-hardened veteran, perhaps a grizzled old senior NCO, and a young, still wet-behind-the-ears, but technology-savvy lieutenant are conducting a dangerous operation. The lieutenant consults his personal data device, which is connected to satellites and ultimately to massive computers back at headquarters. It presents him with all the latest intelligence data, summarized by massive data-mining programs, and the artificial intelligence gives him a probability figure that indicates course of action "A" as likely the most successful approach. The old sergeant respectfully tells his young platoon leader that he has seen this situation several times before and that his instincts tell him that course of action "B" is more likely to accomplish the mission and will result in fewer casualties. The lieutenant, believing his technology, opts for "A" with disastrous results.

Combat is highly unstructured and unpredictable. The enemy's goal is to try to disrupt or deceive our systems. Militaries operate on the basis of trust, with soldiers being critically dependent on their systems and their comrades. They must be able to trust that what they are being told is based on not only good data but good judgment. Important advantages accrue with the use of automated and autonomous systems, not the least of which is that they free humans from doing boring, repetitive, and dangerous jobs and are very efficient in what they do. However, these systems, still somewhat in their infancy, are plagued by some important issues.

An AI system cannot explain in any comprehensible way why it makes the decisions it does. This is antithetical to the military mindset, where it is critical to be able to explain recommendations and to be able to understand, and trust, the system. To be fair, laboratories around the globe are working to improve AI in this regard, but to date we are nowhere near having an AI system that can, in human terms, explain the rationale for its decisions.[36] As a young infantry lieutenant facing Soviet forces along the Fulda Gap in Cold War Germany, I could explain why I deployed my soldiers and vehicles the way I did and describe the logic of my actions to the company or battalion commander. They could either correct my mistake or adopt my tactical reasoning. With AI systems, such explanations are not currently possible. The counterargument is that human decision-making may not be logical or correct either. True enough, but, correct or incorrect, the human cognitive process is at least explainable in human terms.

Next is a worrisome vulnerability to spoofing and false data. AI systems have been reportedly shown to fall prey to adversarial inputs and stray information. Concerns about using AI for lethal decisions are very real. Data manipulation, hacking, and spoofing are problems that have to be solved. Senior Defense Department officials admit that AI systems are really only as good as their training data and that a small amount of corrupted training data could have huge impacts on the predictive ability of such systems.[37] Many AI systems operate with what are known as neural networks in which the computer emulates the neurons of the brain. Operating on billions of pieces of data, the system learns from what it is seeing. But, as with a young child, the learning accomplished is only as good as the data provided. Biased, incomplete, or just plain incorrect data will most likely result in the machine learning the wrong lesson. High-precision weapon systems depend on accurate data for guidance and targeting. Noisy data, where real signals are mixed with and hidden in extraneous signals, can frustrate such systems. Our adversaries know this all too well and will surely exploit this vulnerability.

There are difficulties in adequate testing. How can you test a system if its operation cannot be fully explained or is, by definition, unpredictable? This question then becomes how such systems can be trusted, a concept exceptionally important in military operations. Military testing cannot realistically anticipate, much less replicate, what an enemy will do. AI will inevitably be faced with some enemy behavior for the first time in battle, with unpredictable results.[38] If an operator does not know what an AI will do in a certain situation, it will complicate planning and can make operations more difficult and accidents more likely.[39] Troops in the real world must deal with an adversary's surprise actions, changing weather, and unfamiliar terrain. Unfortunately, AI systems aren't very good at adapting and become ineffective when something significant and unexpected occurs. Humans recognize new experiences and adjust their behavior accordingly. For now, at least, machines must be retrained.[40]

Even more concerning, recent research has shown that if they are not properly designed to prevent such reactions, AI systems can exhibit unexpected learned "aggressive" behavior—as depicted in the scene from Kubrick's movie. Google conducted an experiment where two AI systems were tasked to collect items. When one started losing, it began to employ weapons against the other.[41] Add to this the fact that our national defense strategy itself has become more aggressive, with keywords like *increased lethality* and *defending forward*, and you have the potential for bad behavior by the machines that have to implement in computer code this very strategy. Computer code codifies the algorithms that are, themselves, reflections of the values of the engineers and designers. This raises additional concerns about bias in AI systems and about the ability of a machine to even consider the measured and proportional responses so critical to the laws of armed conflict. Systems designed to win at all costs may not know how to even consider a stalemate or a truce. There is a growing recognition by senior military and intelligence leaders that the training of machine learning systems could introduce unintended biases and that the consequences could be dire.[42]

There is a risk that an adversary's exploitation of our system vulnerabilities might occur faster than humans could react, or might be so subtle as to be undetectable, with the result that control could be ceded nearly completely to the systems, with the human being completely unaware. If the process is so automated as to eliminate the need for human involvement, we must either accept a high level of risk of manipulation by adversaries or ensure that systems are trustworthy and that the possibility of manipulation is mitigated. Completely verifying and securing such complex systems would be nearly impossible, and it would be difficult to build such absolutely trustworthy AI systems. In light of such vulnerabilities, military and civilian war planners must consider the downsides and unknowns before rushing to deploy such technologies.

Another problem is that automated systems, including AI systems, tend to be brittle. They are great at doing what they were designed to do, but they fail miserably when asked to do something different. Notwithstanding the recent Boeing 737 issues, airliners have logged billions of miles with highly automated flight control systems. But the flight regime of an airliner is a relatively well-known and stable situation. In a highly complex battlefield, the data may be like nothing ever seen before, and machine learning systems that depend on good data may be useless.

So the key questions for military planners will be how much trust they place in these technologies and how much control they will actually cede to machines, and under what circumstances. The overarching question about the myriad software, hardware, communications systems, and complex processes remains: Is accurate prediction of their behavior possible? Certainly, no one ever imagined that a missile warning system would mistake the sun's glare for a missile launch, as happened with Lieutenant Colonel Petrov. The global command and control system is not merely complicated; it is more accurately described as a complex adaptive system in which the performance of individual elements may be predictable but the performance of these elements when combined is not. The rapidly approaching implementation of artificial intelligence systems, fraught as they are with technical uncertainties, will make command and control systems even more unpredictable. And what if they can be hacked and the data modified? Experience has shown time and again that very little is safe from a determined hacker. What will happen? The soldiers may not get fed. Airplanes may run out of fuel. Bombs may detonate prematurely. And our antimissile systems may fail to leave the launch pad altogether. In 2007, when Israel bombed Syrian nuclear facilities, it reportedly employed sophisticated cyber techniques to pump the Syrian air defense sensors full of useless data and bogus commands.[43] Syrian air defenses simply did not work. Antiaircraft missiles never left their launchers.

What kind of mistakes might an autonomous command and control system make, and what might be the ramifications? The answer, of course, depends on where in the command and control chain such an error occurs. It could be simple (but nonetheless important), serious, or catastrophic. Take, for example, a mission-planning system that uses a purpose-directed AI system to determine the logistics needs of deployed soldiers, perhaps calculating the needs of soldiers for ammunition on the basis of historical expenditure rates. Such a calculation might fail to anticipate an out-of-the blue, unexpectedly ferocious firefight and put soldiers at risk of running out of ammunition when they most need it. Another serious issue might occur if an AI system falls prey to hacking and adversarial inputs. For instance, an adversary may be able to insert credible fake data into our sensors and target recognition systems, making us think a target is real when it is, in fact, innocent noncombatants. The Stuxnet attack on Iranian centrifuges was especially sophisticated, as it reportedly was able to insert data to convince operators that everything was fine while the centrifuges were destroying themselves. Finally, a catastrophic issue might occur if an AI-controlled decision support system is confused by an absence of data or by unexpected data, or if it automatically determines that any perceived aggression must be met with a similar or more aggressive response, when in fact a de-escalation is called for.

The US military and other militaries around the world are racing to incorporate AI into their weapons systems, lest the adversary gain an advantage. Fair enough, but military units need to first understand the potential issues of such a rush to field the technology. Errors in individual systems may have minimal or manageable risk, but when they are combined with other AI systems, likely employing different algorithms, answers may be confusing and inconsistent. The greatest risks posed by military applications of AI—increasingly autonomous weapons, and algorithmic command and control—are that the interactions between the systems deployed will be extremely complex, impossible to model, and subject to catastrophic forms of failure that are hard to predict, much less mitigate. As a result, there is a serious risk of accidental conflict, or accidental escalation of conflict, if machine learning or algorithmic automation is used in these kinds of military applications.

Russia reportedly had, or has, a system known as "the Dead Hand."[44] Dead Hand was a Cold War–era automatic nuclear weapons-control system used by the Soviet Union. An example of fail-deadly and mutually assured destruction deterrence, it could automatically trigger the launch of the Russian intercontinental ballistic missiles (ICBMs) if a nuclear strike was detected by sensors, even with the commanding elements fully destroyed. By most accounts, it was normally switched off and was supposed to be activated during dangerous crises only; however, it is said to remain fully functional and able to serve its purpose whenever it may be needed. A system known as the AN/DRC-8 Emergency Rocket Communications System (ERCS) existed in the US.[45] ERCS was decommissioned in 1991.

Incredibly, two American academics—former military officers—suggest that it may be necessary for the US to take advantage of the benefits of artificial intelligence and recreate for the US a "Dead Hand" system: "It may be necessary to develop a system *based on artificial intelligence*, with predetermined response decisions, that detects, decides, and directs strategic forces with such speed that the attack-time compression challenge does not place the United States in an impossible position."[46] What a frightening proposition! With all the uncertainties inherent in AI systems and the enormity of a decision to engage in nuclear combat, a rational person has to question if they were really serious or if they merely intended to be provocative. Fortunately, at least for now the director of the Defense Department's artificial intelligence development office has explicitly ruled out incorporating AI into the nuclear command and control system.[47] Given that elements of the system are continually in need of modernization and upgrade, however, it is not at all clear that some forms of AI will not eventually creep into some portions of the nuclear command and control infrastructure. Nuclear systems are the major worry, but no one has ruled out the use of AI in non-nuclear command and control systems. While the dangers may not be so potentially catastrophic, they are, nonetheless, real and potentially fatal. As a RAND Corporation report concluded, "The multiparty arms race in the domain of machine learning and AI will continue to pose risks to all sides—and it is unclear how to mitigate them."[48]

The use of artificial intelligence in weapon systems and their command and control raises new questions of morality and ethics. As the speed of war increases and the demands on human operators grow, humans will have to rely more heavily on AI. The ethical principles programmed by the developer or learned by the system—with whatever bias they represent—will influence the system's "moral" choices.[49] In the end, however, it is not the machine but the human commander who has the responsibility and must be the moral agent.

Do these new weapons actually increase the possibility of war? If so, how? An automated decision by an AI-controlled command and control system might raise questions of proper authority. It seems ridiculous on its face to assert that a machine can be considered a "proper authority." If AI systems continue to be unexplainable in human terms, as they currently are, how would we be able to determine if the decision to go to war was one of last resort? Large-scale software systems are designed and largely built by humans. If a system cannot properly explain itself, there is no way to be sure the answers it provides are free of bias.[50] How then can we determine if the decision to go to war was made with right, unbiased, intention? We cannot wait, as we did in the past, to employ these systems first and then figure out how we might control them. It will be critical to figure out these questions before we stumble into a war in which we may find that control is impossible.

Ethical issues are discussed in official studies of AI but, unfortunately, do not rank high on the list of priorities for those interested in military applications. The Department of Defense Innovation Board (DIB) recently released a set of draft rules on the ethical use of AI that several leading researchers called a good start, but they are, to emphasize, only guidelines. A bipartisan commission established by the 2019 National Defense Authorization Act said that the US military should not let debates over ethics and human control "paralyze AI development."[51] Further, the US chief technology officer criticized the European Union's more prescriptive efforts, saying that the US prefers a lighter regulatory touch or "limited regulatory overreach."[52]

Military forces are deployed all over the world. They are heavily armed and highly networked. They depend on massive amounts of data, collected from an enormous number of sensors, linked to multiple computer systems in widely distributed command centers. They are stretched thin and are under enormous stress. War and weapons have changed in fundamental ways, and so rapidly as to sometimes seem vertiginous. Dual-use technologies have allowed actors formerly unable to compete to threaten developed world powers. Military superpowers invest heavily in sophisticated, lethal, high-speed, computer-controlled weaponry. Antagonists seem to be everywhere and more heavily armed than ever. Militaries consist of both people and machines. Human behavior is notoriously unpredictable, and a growing dependence on machines that employ computers and artificial intelligence is making it even more so. Militaries are complex adaptive systems that will modify their behavior in response to their environment. They are probabilistic in nature. So what we have is a very uncertain, ambiguous, and unstable environment.

UNSTABLE EQUILIBRIUM AND CATASTROPHIC REACTIONS

Seemingly small events during times of crisis can cascade into large misunderstandings and, ultimately, war. The military is highly dependent on automation, sensors, data, communications, cyber capabilities, and space systems. It depends on high-tech weapons that are increasingly unpredictable in their behavior. The enormous operations pressure and the dependence on technology make it vulnerable and prone to error. A world bristling with weapons, led by strident and militarily obsessed politicians and despots, in which countries face one another over highly contentious issues and grievances, can only be described as full of pent-up energy and dangerously unstable.

In physics and mathematics, the concept of unstable equilibrium is an important one. In its most basic definition, *unstable equilibrium* means that if a system is pushed one way on either side of an equilibrium point, the motion will accelerate *away* from equilibrium as a means of lowering the energy. In the physics of phase transformations, there is a concept known as nucleation in which, for example, superheated water will, if disturbed, explosively create bubbles in an attempt to lower the energy of the system. The overwhelming "desire" of a system is to get to a lower energy, less excited, state. Just as in physics, where unstable equilibrium can be disturbed by a change in local energy balances, so too can a fragile global peace be upset by a seemingly minor event. The notion of the world situation as a global pressure cooker, in which a disturbance or imperfection somewhere could create a high-energy event, is a compelling one. At the moment, an uneasy—unstable—equilibrium exists around the world. If the buildup of pressure is great, the resulting release of pressure could be catastrophic.

In physical structures, a high degree of connectedness more easily transmits shock. The physics of solids, for instance, tells us that the higher the elastic modulus of a solid, the stiffer it is, and the faster a wave will travel through it. The more tightly connected the elements of a system are, the easier it is for an impulse in one part of a system to be felt in a distant part of the system. A provocative action by an adversary or a mistake somewhere in our globally deployed military could quickly ricochet through the system and escalate. Clearly, these analogies are not perfect but merely represent the highly complex and unpredictable nature of interactions among highly energetic systems. They remind us that once a process or a change of physical state begins, it is often difficult or impossible to stop. Just as in a physical system where there may be a rapid and sometimes explosive decompression, so too a military situation may devolve into such behavior.

Today, the degree of global interconnectivity is breathtaking. Shots fired in one place truly can be heard around the world—with immediate reaction. Events occurring in one place can affect almost instantaneously the performance of systems in other, distant places. A former CIA colleague wrote that "our world today is an information ecology, rich with complex interdependencies, in which the decisions or actions of one agency, institution, or nation affect others in complex, frequently unanticipated, ways."[53] Outcomes from complex interactions are impossible to predict. Shocks in one part of a highly networked system can cascade uncontrollably.[54]

Military technologies can spin out of control because of errors by their creators, by operational users, or from unintended interactions of the technologies themselves.[55] Today's systems are just too large and complex and the number of people involved in developing and fielding them are too numerous to ensure that they are error free. Complex systems tend to fail in complex ways. Systems will fail, and we cannot even begin to predict how they will do so. The overall global trend is toward high-tech, highly automated warfare, with humans becoming less important. Add to this the fact that automated and AI-controlled command and control systems are increasingly unpredictable, and the uncertainty and instability increase further still.

Americans have long been fascinated by technology and weapons, even though they understand little about them. We are living in an era in which technology advances come so fast that we barely have time to integrate one into our daily lives before another is upon us. That we think technology development is more rapid than ever before is not an illusion. A look at technology adoption rates over the last century shows that new technologies appear at a faster rate and are integrated over a shorter period of time.[56] Americans thrive on technology; we are seduced by it and addicted to a never-ending stream of innovations. This has been true almost from the country's founding. There have always been new technologies introduced in warfare that have made militaries faster, more lethal, or better able to communicate. Indeed, the US military has moved increasingly toward substituting advanced weapons for personnel—technology instead of blood—in its quest for superiority and its desire to minimize casualties among its soldiers.[57] What is different now? In the past, advanced technologies were implemented in modest numbers of weapons. Today, technology is pervasive and is available to soldiers even in the lowest echelons of battle units. Technology promises to make war more deadly and efficient but also to supplement, and ultimately replace, human judgment and decision-making.

The numerous human urges to violence, the computerized nature of militaries, the sophistication of weapons, and the new, more aggressive posture of the most highly armed countries create a dangerous situation, a sort of unstable equilibrium in which an unexpected event could precipitate a failure and a resort to conflict. We are exceedingly fortunate that major conflicts among the great powers have not yet occurred. However, in a world bristling with deadly weapons both old and new, with antagonism between countries facing one another in tense situations around the globe, we must find ways to control our urges to violence.

T W O

———————●———————

URGES TO VIOLENCE

Thus, it happens that those who have force on loan
from fate count on it too much and are destroyed.
—Simone Weil, *The Iliad, or the Poem of Force*, 1939

What are the things that lead us so often to resort to force? Many of
the urges to violence have always been a part of relationships between
countries. The fascination with technology and superweapons, the influence of the arms industry, the ubiquity and power of the media, a
lack of education, competition for resources, and nationalism and religious and ethnic hatreds are some of the well-known influences on
war and violent conflict.

What is different now is that these urges are aided and abetted,
and sometimes magnified, by the availability of new technologies.
Time frames are shortened dramatically, weapons operate at greater
distances, antagonists can remain anonymous, and the cost of some

weapons no longer presents a barrier to entry. What might lead countries to break through the restraints that have held them in check to date? Ultimately, what might we do to keep those urges in check?

FASCINATION WITH TECHNOLOGY
AND SUPERWEAPONS

In late nineteenth-century America, progress came to be measured by advances in technology. Historian Perry Miller was the first to note the sense of rapture that early American citizens sometimes demonstrated at the introduction of new technologies. People often responded as if seeing technological marvels was something of a spiritual experience. He found that technological advancements created in the public mind a sort of religious reverence. Miller referred to this as the "technological sublime."[1]

David Nye, also a historian of technology, followed up on Miller's concept of the technological sublime, describing the awe and trepidation that many Americans felt with the introduction of new technological advances of the time. Simply put, technologies evoke collective awe and amazement and inspire the imagination. Nye felt that this experience and the widespread belief in the notion of inevitable progress formed a distinctly American ideology of technology. He noted that in America technological achievements became measures of cultural value.[2] He concluded that the almost-religious feelings evoked by technology, when combined with America's view of its messianic destiny, created a kind of American nationalism, providing a shared set of experiences around which the national character could coalesce.[3] Even the greatest human problems, Americans thought, could be solved by our technological genius.

The fascination of Americans with technology naturally extended to weapons. The philosopher Edmund Burke claimed that "whatever is fitted in any sort to excite the ideas of pain and danger, that is to say, whatever is in any sort terrible . . . or operates in a manner analogous to terror, is a source of the sublime."[4] The public and our civilian and military leaders are seduced by technology and its progeny, superweapons. Unfortunately, such superweapons also seduce us into thinking we are invincible. One researcher noted that "innovation makes policy makers swoon and weapons developers salivate."[5] Countries and governments have always used the possibility of "superweapons" to awe and inspire their own populations and to frighten and deter their adversaries. The ancient Greeks had rudimentary flamethrowers, the Chinese perfected the crossbow in the fifth century BC, Germany introduced guided missiles and cruise missiles in the Second World War, and, of course, the US had a brief monopoly on nuclear weapons.

In his book *War Stars*, professor H. Bruce Franklin describes the technology-worshipping culture of the nineteenth century as shaping the collective imagination of a future dominated by superweapons. He writes that the emerging faith in technological genius combined with the widespread view of America's messianic destiny "engendered a cult of made-in-America superweapons and ecstatic visions of America defeating evil empires, waging wars to end all wars, and making the world safe for democracy. Looming above all, no matter who the imagined enemy, appear avatars of the superweapon in terribly modern and familiar shapes."[6] Americans have always been fascinated with weapons of mass destruction. Franklin notes that since the seventeenth century, many Americans have believed they lived on the brink of the apocalypse. The literature of the eighteenth and nineteenth centuries included a long list of books describing the future destruction of the country by better-armed foreign nations and the need for America to have fantastic new weapons to prevent it. A particularly relevant example is Stanley Waterloo's 1898 book *Armageddon: A Tale of Love, War, and Invention,* in which the hero of the novel says, "To have a world at peace there must be massed in the controlling nations such power of destruction as may not even be questioned. So, we shall build our appliances of destruction, calling to our aid every discovery and achievement of science."[7] In the present day, we have some writers expressing the same sentiments. One conservative educator, appealing to the aforementioned apocalyptic fears, says, "The time is now for every American to demand a national policy of clear-cut military superiority. Every American is threatened. Every American has a stake in our own survival. We have passed from superiority to sufficiency to insufficiency. Irretrievability is just a short time away. Our nation must be summoned to this challenge and this is one challenge that must be met if America is to enter its third century as a free and powerful nation."[8] Note the sense of impending doom.

In March 1983, President Ronald Reagan proposed a missile shield that would render Soviet ballistic missiles ineffective.[9] Though it was widely viewed by scientists as a fantasy, dependent on technologies in very early stages of development and decades away from maturity, the public nonetheless believed it. Some missile defense zealots still believe that the Strategic Defense Initiative convinced the Soviet Union they could not prevail over the US and thus ended the Cold War.

In 1986, I and my fellow officers in the small Pentagon office of the Strategic Defense Initiative worked for days crafting a mere handful of words for President Reagan's State of the Union speech in which he would announce the development of a hypersonic airplane that would move passengers around the world at enormous speeds. If successful, the project also had potential for use as an antisatellite weapon or weapon delivery vehicle, as confirmed by the Defense Science Board in 1992.[10] However, former Lockheed Skunk Works legendary engineer Ben Rich would say that he doubted the system could be built in fifty years, much less the then-advertised three years, and that whoever had dreamed up the president's speech should be canned![11]

Then, as now, we have leaders boasting about their military capabilities in an attempt to deter adversaries. They become seduced by weapons technology. The danger of this seduction is that we will actually begin to believe our own boasting and think that all of what we know about war will be rendered obsolete by fantastic new weapons.[12] Former Harvard president Drew Faust traced the seductiveness of war to its location on the "boundary of the human, the inhuman, and the superhuman," saying it offers "the attraction of the extraordinary."[13] In the present day, consider nuclear weapons. It is well known that the scientists and engineers who built the first bombs were seduced by the "elegance" of the physics and were awestruck by the enormous power of the weapons, which aroused both excitement and existential dread.

The seduction metaphor is particularly relevant to technology and weapons. Seduction of an individual begins with the allure of something exciting and attractive that gives great satisfaction. The object of desire somehow promises immediate benefit and instant gratification.

The dangers and possibilities of unknown consequences, of course, are too often overlooked in the "heat of the moment." Negative consequences are downplayed or ignored—or simply explained away.

In the mid-1970s, I commanded a US Army nuclear weapons depot in Europe whose mission was to store and perform maintenance on many hundreds of tactical nuclear weapons for use by NATO allies in the event the USSR decided to invade western Europe. It was my duty to release these weapons on properly authenticated command from the commander in chief. As a relatively young officer I was struck by the enormity of the mission and, in truth, proud to have been vested with such awesome responsibility. Deep in the back of my mind, however, was always the realization of the horror the weapons would create, and every notification of an incoming coded message from headquarters created a slight shiver of dread. I rationalized.

Three decades later, as a senior officer, I was granted rare access to the detailed engineering and inner workings of modern nuclear weapons. Like the inventors and early engineers, I was awestruck by the deep understanding of physics and the innovation and clever engineering employed in this new generation of devices. However, when you are standing inside the cavernous rooms of a deeply buried and highly secure weapon storage facility, the sight of seemingly endless rows and stacks of megaton-class thermonuclear warheads has a psychological impact that cannot be dismissed. Rationalization became infinitely more difficult.

A DOUBLE-EDGED SWORD

Science fiction writers like H. G. Wells imagined fantastic, magical new weapons like particle beams and even atomic bombs. Little did these writers know that such types of weapons would become reality years later. British science fiction author Arthur C. Clarke famously said, "Any sufficiently advanced technology is indistinguishable from magic."[14] We should worry, however, that the possession of such magic can become a double-edged sword:

The wise old sorcerer and his young apprentice toiled away together all day, with the old man conjuring up spells for many people and many purposes. The young man watched and listened eagerly, thinking, "This doesn't seem so hard; I have seen what the boss does and I can do it myself." When the sorcerer departed his workshop, he left the apprentice with chores to perform. Tired of fetching water by pail, the apprentice enchanted a broom to do the work for him, using magic he thought he remembered adequately but did not. Soon there was a flood, and the apprentice realized he could not control the broom because he did not know how. When he tried to split the broom, it only doubled the rush of water.

Just when all seemed lost, the old sorcerer returned. He quickly broke the spell and lectured the apprentice, saying that only a master should invoke powerful spirits.

The unmistakable message of "The Sorcerer's Apprentice" is that humans can have command of awesome powers without any true mastery of those powers.[15] Command is one thing, mastery quite another. Technology is like magic. In untrained hands or inadequately understood, it can get away from us and cause problems. Consider research on deadly pathogens, for example. Without detailed knowledge of how such pathogens propagate—and how to stop them—research on them is extremely dangerous, and once such pathogens escape, they may be uncontrollable.

When Prometheus stole fire from heaven, Zeus, the king of the gods, took vengeance by presenting Pandora to Prometheus's brother Epimetheus, telling him that he should marry Pandora, and he also sent Pandora a little box with the instructions never to open it. Very curious about what was in the box, Pandora stole the key from Epimetheus and opened the box. It was filled with

all manner of ills and evils, which escaped into the world before
Pandora could close it. Only hope remained inside.

The story of Pandora is a tale of excessive curiosity even in the face of warnings about the dangers of exploring things we are aware may hurt us.[16] Certainly, nuclear weapons were an evil released upon the world. Are we now opening Pandora's box with a new generation of weapons that might escape our control? Once released into the wild, can they be put back into the box? Writing about the future of warfare, the author Henry Adams said, "I firmly believe that before many centuries more, science will be the master of man. The engines he will have invented will be beyond his strength to control. Someday science may have the existence of mankind in its power, and the human race commit suicide, by blowing up the world."[17]

Current writers on the dangers of artificial intelligence point to the fact that it is by its nature not understandable or predictable. Even our sorcerers may not be able to control it, much less our apprentices. Writers discussing nuclear weapons often lament the fact that the nuclear "genie is out of the bottle" and cannot be put back in, that nuclear weapons cannot be uninvented. The questions for us now are important. What are the "magic" technologies? Who understands them well enough to play the role of the sorcerer? How well trained are the apprentices? Are our apprentices ready and do they understand enough about how the technologies work to employ them properly? Can the sorcerer, in fact, stop the magic, or will it have an intelligence of its own? Can any of the potential bad side effects be put back in the box once released?

There are other negative effects of our dependence on a continued supply of new technologies. In the latest version of the *Global Trends* reports, the director of national intelligence concludes that the rate of technological progress is creating new opportunities but also causing discontinuities and aggravating divisions between winners and losers. Automation and artificial intelligence, they say, will change industries faster than economies can adjust, displacing workers and inhibiting development in the poorest countries.[18] The same report notes that the risk of future conflict will increase because of, among other things, *the spread of lethal, disruptive technologies.* Such disruption will become easier and more common, with technology to create weapons of mass destruction becoming more accessible to more groups, many with little knowledge and few compunctions about their use. We have already seen armed drones deployed by nonstate actors in conflicts in Ukraine and recently in an attack on an oil refinery in Saudi Arabia. Bioweapons capabilities continue to proliferate. Relatively fast and inexpensive genetic manipulation and virus-editing techniques are readily available to a growing number of laboratories and individuals around the world.[19] Technology, it seems, is abetting many of the worst human behaviors and creating some of its biggest dangers.

TECHNOLOGY GONE MAD

The industrialization of warfare so evident in the massive killing and destruction of World War I and the unprecedented involvement of scientists and engineers so evident in the advanced weapons of World War II, including the atomic bomb, caused many writers and philosophers to raise questions about the moral responsibilities of engineers and scientists. In the aftermath of the bombing of Nagasaki, Japan, the philosopher Jacob Bronowski wrote that "because we know how gunpowder works, we sigh for the days before atomic bombs. But massacre is not prevented by gunpowder. . . . Massacre is prevented by the scientist's ethic . . . that the end for which we work exists and is judged only by the means which we use to reach it."[20]

In accepting the Nobel Prize for literature in 1957, philosopher and former member of the French Resistance Albert Camus said, "My generation's task . . . consists in preventing the world from destroying itself. Heir to a corrupt history, in which are mingled fallen revolutions, and *technology gone mad . . . where intelligence has debased itself to become the servant of hatred and oppression*, this generation has had to reestablish a little of that which constitutes the dignity of life and death."[21]

The philosopher Isaiah Berlin approached the fascination with technology somewhat obliquely, cautioning against a too-slavish obedience to the wonders of technological solutions.[22] He worried that "the vision of some future perfection, as in the minds of technocrats in our own time," would be used to justify barbarous behavior by rulers against their own people. Berlin felt that some leaders had been convinced, on the basis of the experiences of large-scale administrative states, the advanced mechanization and industrialization of everything in society, and the limitless potential of science, that they could devise a system of governing in which all values must be compatible and that, in the end, there is some grand solution that will incorporate them all. He was including in his argument those for whom technology played an outsized role in their visions of a perfect future. This had led, Berlin believed, to heinous, oppressive regimes. Writing in 1958, Berlin clearly had in mind the excesses of the Nazi regime and Stalinist Russia.

In Germany, Goethe's *Faust* was loved by scientists as well as the general public well into the twentieth century and was considered by most Germans to be a canonical text. *Faust* inspired German scientists to search for a "single, coherent, picture of the world encompassing all phenomena, constants, laws, and concepts."[23] As Albert Speer, armaments minister of the Third Reich, said, "Hitler's dictatorship differed in one fundamental point from all its predecessors in history. His was the first dictatorship in the present period of technical development, a dictatorship which made complete use of all technical means for the domination of its own country."[24]

THE GLOBAL ARMS INDUSTRY

Among other things, the excessive militarism and the proclivity toward war in many countries are fueled by the ready availability of modern weapons. The global arms industry anxiously awaits a continuous flow of new-technology weapons and plays a large and central role in ensuring a continuous supply of such weapons. They invite a resort to armed conflict.

You enter the sprawling compound, often near a civilian or military airport, and are immediately awed by the displays of gleaming or camouflage-painted advanced military aircraft, mobile rocket launchers, and transportable radar systems, too large to fit inside a building. Private security guards stand watch over the multi-million-dollar equipment but are genial and invite onlookers and potential buyers to examine the merchandise. Upon entering the convention center or other large venue, you are immediately struck by the large number and variety of vendors and pieces of military hardware and the spare-no-expense nature of the event. You are greeted and offered giveaways, like pens or flashlights with corporate logos, to get you to stop and view a display. Companies offering their products include large international defense firms and smaller second- and third-tier suppliers. Huge systems are there alongside little things like night vision devices, new combat uniforms, small arms, and even military rations. Sometimes referred to as defense industry trade shows, these events are, in fact, arms bazaars.

The global arms industry promises awesome new power for national leaders. Its never-ending warnings about adversary capability growth encourage an arms race and raise the possibility of use of such large stocks of weapons. Now with the return of so-called great power competition, the manufacture and sale of not only new, dual-use technologies but also big-ticket items are more lucrative than ever.

The defense industry and Silicon Valley companies have an outsized influence on policy and economic contributions to national economies. They will send representatives and lobbyists to Congress to meet with lawmakers in classified sessions to tell them of the systems on which foreign companies and governments are working. In 2018, the defense industry employed over seven hundred lobbyists and spent $126 million on lobbying.[25] Lobbyists will urgently warn that we're back to great power competition, that we're in danger of falling behind, and that we have to be ready to fight and win a major war with Russia and China. The idea of peer-competitor conflicts benefits the defense industry, implying the need for and encouraging the purchase of big, expensive weapons.

Total global military expenditure rose to $1.9 trillion in 2019, according to new data from the Stockholm International Peace Research

Institute (SIPRI). This represents an increase of 3.6 percent from 2018 and was the largest annual growth in spending since 2010. Military expenditures by the United States grew by 5.3 percent to a total of $732 billion in 2019 and accounted for 38 percent of global military spending. China was the second-largest military spender in the world, with expenditures of $261 billion, a 5.1 percent increase compared with 2018. The US remained by far the largest spender in the world, with a military budget larger than those of the next seven countries combined. In 2019 Russia was the fourth-largest spender in the world and increased its military expenditure by 4.5 percent to $65.1 billion. At 3.9 percent of its GDP, Russia's military spending burden was among the highest in Europe. Data from 2018 showed that globally, aerospace and defense industry profits climbed 9 percent as defense spending continued to rise across the globe.[26] Defense firms in the US reported a 6 percent increase in profits, while European firms reported a whopping 21 percent increase.[27] Of consequence, in 2016 the CEOs of nine of the top ten US defense firms each made between $15 and $20 million.[28]

Profiteering got so bad during World War I that a congressional inquiry into the behavior of the arms industry confirmed that private weapons firms had "fomented war scares, bribed government officials, and circulated false, inflammatory reports on various nations' military strength, to stimulate arms spending."[29] While there is no suggestion here of such scurrilous behavior today, President Dwight Eisenhower's often-quoted exhortation, in his farewell speech to the nation, to guard against the influence of the "military-industrial complex" remains appropriate. Eisenhower was highly critical of the aerospace industry and the military for their unending demand for more weapons. He was reportedly angered by the industry press advocating for more weapons to meet an ever-bigger and better Soviet threat that they had "conjured up" and was outraged by the air force officers, industry lobbyists, trade associations, and congressmen shamelessly promoting arms purchases.[30] Andrew Bacevich says, "Judged 50 years later, Ike's frightening prophecy actually understates the scope of the modern system—and the dangers of the perpetual march to war it has put us on."[31]

As Jonathan Caverley points out, the link between heavily capitalized militaries and increasingly aggressive behavior is strong, with an increase in any measure of capitalization resulting in an increased probability of aggression.[32] In a somewhat arcane but interesting calculation, he concludes from the historical data that a one-standard-deviation increase in average defense spending results in a fourfold increase in the risk of military aggression.[33] Research, development, acquisition, and sale of weapons at home and around the world have become significant elements of the American economy, causing politicians to be very cautious about standing in the way of military adventures.[34] Multiple studies have shown that politicians frequently manipulate defense spending for political gain and that corporate actors have a powerful influence on such spending.[35] In a new take on the classic saying that to a hammer everything looks like a nail, commentator Dennis Wille said, "If all you've got is a defense strategy looking at weapons, how are you *not* going to get there?"

While we may be tempted to think this worry about huge arms budgets and large militaries is a modern-war concern, scholars and statesmen have worried about just this phenomenon for centuries. In the sixteenth, seventeenth, and eighteenth centuries, European manufacturers sold firearms all over the world. The nineteenth century saw the emergence of major arms conglomerates like Krupp in Germany, Schneider-Creusot in France, and Vickers in Britain.[36] The eighteenth-century philosopher Immanuel Kant noted the dangers. In his 1795 masterpiece "Perpetual Peace," he warned that "wars would grow increasingly violent and periods of peace would become more burdened by rearmament and by hostile policies that would *lead to further conflict*."[37] Even the Vatican criticized the rush to arms. An 1870 document, the *Postulata* of Vatican Council I, said that the very size of national military establishments created an "intolerable burden" on society and created a *propensity to make them pay for themselves through conquest*, leading to wars the church should not treat as just wars.[38] In 1898, Tsar Nicholas II wrote that "massive systems of armament are transforming the armed peace of our days into a crushing burden. If the incessant building of arms is allowed to continue *it will inevitably lead to the cataclysm* which it is desired to avert."[39] In the twenty years prior to World War I, Britain, France, Germany, Russia, and Austria-Hungary began building up their military power. Spending on arms increased dramatically and accompanied a parallel dramatic increase in nationalism in which each country felt that the best way to reveal its superiority was to create a stronger military. In World War II, the mere existence of the atomic bomb is thought by some to have been a key factor in the decision to actually use it.

General George C. Marshall, who was awarded the Nobel Peace Prize in 1953, was a proponent both of a necessary military strength and of peace. He argued in his acceptance speech that the maintenance of large armies was not a good basis for policy and that a large military, however necessary, was too limited a foundation on which to build a long-enduring peace.[40] Marshall also held that massive imbalances in weapons and military power were dangerous and destabilizing and implied the need for attempts at arms control. Such self-restraint from dominance seeking by developed countries has obviously not occurred and is not now occurring with the new generation of weapons and technologies.

COMPETITION FOR RESOURCES AND CLIMATE CHANGE

Rapid population growth combined with climate change is putting pressure on food, water, and other natural resources, resulting in increased human migration and a corresponding resistance to that migration by established populations. Resource competition is fierce and will worsen over time. As the world skyrockets toward eight billion inhabitants or more, as climate patterns change, and as resource scarcities arise, the probability of violence rises.

Global scarcity of vital natural resources and climate change are likely to produce unrest, rebellion, competition, and conflict.[41] The director of national intelligence, in the report *Global Trends 2025,* has said unequivocally that chronic food and water shortages will assume increasing importance for a growing number of countries during the next fifteen to twenty years and has concluded that climate change and resource scarcity are looming future threats to national security on a level of severity along with terror and nuclear proliferation.[42] The US Army Special Operations Command's new strategy recognizes and plans for the fact that climate change will affect global demographics and economies and will drive political instability and resource competition.[43] A report by the Center for Naval Analysis has concluded that climate change will be a concern for military forces as it acts as a threat multiplier for instability in volatile parts of the world.[44] Historians point to repeated patterns in which ancient civilizations experienced war and conflict over the scarcity of resources brought on by overpopulation, drought, and crop failures.[45] Food shortages and resource scarcity have contributed to the onset of war, or the continuation of it, for centuries. The Thirty Years' War was not only about differences in religious belief but also about class hatreds, differences in culture, and even competition for scarce foodstuffs.[46] That conflict left eight million casualties, not only from battles, but from famine and disease.[47] Others have pointed to modern conflicts based on the unmet demand for food and other commodities, such as the 1931 Japanese invasion of Manchuria.[48]

Rapid population growth in developing countries will itself put pressure on these vital resources. The stress on resources will be made worse by climate change, the physical effects of which will worsen throughout this period, with changing rainfall patterns and water scarcities harming agriculture in many parts of the globe. Brought on, in part, by unconstrained technology development and industrialization, climate change is now contributing to crop failures, water shortages, and starvation, leading to population migration. Climate change is reducing the availability of water in some regions by as much as a third, affecting food production. By midcentury, two hundred million people may be permanently displaced as "climate migrants."[49] The United Nations has estimated that drought and overpopulation contributed to the violence that killed or wounded between three hundred thousand and five hundred thousand people and displaced more than two million in Darfur.[50] In 2011, food shortages and high prices led to deadly tribal wars in Ethiopia.[51] The UN has reported that over the last sixty years, 40 percent of civil wars can be associated with natural resources, and since 1990 at least eighteen violent conflicts have been fueled or financed by natural resources. Natural resources may also relate to violent conflict in second-order ways such as the displacement of populations into fragile environments where the struggle to survive degrades the resource base.[52]

Nationalist sentiment is a form of national pride and national belonging based on political, ethnic, and cultural beliefs, combined with a belief in the superiority of one's nation. It is also often closely aligned with racism. In highly nationalistic societies, people are told that other cultures or people from other countries are morally and intellectually inferior. Xenophobia is a negative attitude toward, or fear of, individuals or groups who are in some sense different. It is prejudiced against, and vilifies, people who are deemed outsiders or foreigners. Xenophobia is closely related to nationalism. At their most extreme, nationalism, xenophobia, racism, and ethnic and religious hatreds can move individuals and groups to try to eliminate those who are different by perpetrating violence against them.[53] The mass migration of refugees seeking a better, more predictable life for themselves and their families is creating stress on established communities. Large influxes of foreign citizens place pressure on existing civil and social structures, and for some elements of those existing communities their presence is seen as creating a zero-sum situation.

In the years before World War I, nationalist fervor in Europe was at a high pitch. The continent had become "infected with an inflated sense of *patriotism and xenophobia* which fueled an alarmingly intensive arms race."[54] In the US, patriotism became viciously xenophobic, with even the government fomenting animosity toward people who were "different."[55] In World War II, extreme xenophobia was directed against Americans of Japanese descent. And, in the aftermath of 9/11, American citizens of Middle Eastern and Muslim backgrounds were subjected to severe discrimination and violence. In Europe, there has been a long-term trend in rising nationalist parties making significant gains in parliamentary elections.[56]

Sadly, this is not just a modern phenomenon. In ancient Rome, there was a widespread belief that "traditional values" were being undermined by foreign immigrants, among them, "slippery and corrupt Greeks" who had come to Rome.[57] This sounds depressingly similar to our current situation. In the coming years, populism, nationalism, xenophobia, and anti-immigrant sentiment, fueled by instant communication, will increase as demographic trends intensify. Extremist leaders will resort to nationalistic and religious rhetoric to incite their followers. The sad fact is that religion does play a role in violence, contributing to arguments for war and providing impetus to the eruption of conflict.[58] Nationalism and theological fanaticism will be, as Bertrand Russell said about what he called "organized party spirit," "one of the greatest dangers of our time."[59] Radical extremist groups, be they foreign or homegrown, constantly repeat and circulate apocalyptic, xenophobic, or nationalistic ideologies that act as rallying cries to susceptible individuals. These groups believe that outside forces are conspiring against them somehow, that there is an existential threat to their way of life—most often caused by people who are "different" —and that the only way to ensure self-preservation is to use violence.

Then there is excessive patriotism, closely related to nationalism. Patriotism in its proper form is an important emotion, as it represents a rational pride in one's country. However, excessive patriotism, along with its sibling militarism, is the worship of national power that knows no limits to its assertion.[60] Nobel Peace Prize recipient Jane Addams felt that patriotism when equated with national power and support for the military was much too narrow of a conception for such an important emotion. She wrote that patriotism was based too much on past military prowess and that while we might admire a past life of courageous warfare, we should not accord it the right to dominate the present.[61]

Reinhold Niebuhr described the dangers of uncritical patriotism, explaining that individually unselfish patriotism, when combined with that of the populace, evolves into a rabid nationalism. The fervor often becomes so strong that individuals cease to be critical or questioning of their government. As he so correctly—and frighteningly—pointed out, "The unqualified character of this devotion is the very basis of the nation's power and of the freedom to use that power without moral restraint."[62] Russian writer Leo Tolstoy felt that patriotic fervor was a powerful form of propaganda and that governments used it to incite and justify their decisions to go to war.[63] If more citizens were critically questioning the behavior of their governments, they might find that their emotions were being manipulated and might not utter such trite phrases as "my country right or wrong."[64] This critical stance would not be disloyalty, just not blind loyalty.

THE MEDIA'S MULTIPLE ROLES

The media, in all their forms (print, radio, television, social media, etc.) play multiple, often conflicting roles in militarism and the decisions of a nation to go to war. In some cases, they act as a tool of the government, in others as a critic, but because war and peace are so important to nations, the media are always interested and involved.

While the commonly held view of the role of the media as the "Fourth Estate" is that media have a responsibility to challenge the necessity or the given rationale for resorting to violence, they often do just the opposite. Too frequently, the media become supporters of the decision to resort to war. As Susan Carruthers writes, "Just when deliberative democracy cries out for vigorous debate, media may seem at their most supine and credulous."[65] She points out that when the media rightfully question the wisdom of political leaders, or appear too sympathetic to innocent civilians in the war zone, the public will often rebuke them for failing to display sufficient support for "our troops."

The press, for mostly market-based reasons, is not really very good at informing citizens about international affairs. Foreign policy coverage tends to be uncritical, especially in the run-up to and early stages of war.[66] Always on in this era of twenty-four-hour coverage, the media record actions and transmit information and images without context, often with language meant to incite. The media—print, television, radio, internet, social media—add to the possibility of violence in several ways. Potential warring factions use the media, now faster than ever before, to urge their followers to violence. The media have historically played a large role in inciting war fervor among populations. Peace and harmony do not sell. They are boring.

Media reporting often lacks context or worse, accuracy, and includes graphic photographs and stories in an attempt to capture the public's attention, provoking demands for action. American military and foreign policy that develops to address popular emotional responses provoked by commercial media skews or diminishes the role of the normal processes of government. When the public is seeing events as they happen, they are likely to demand that policy makers respond rapidly. Time for reflection may be squeezed to the point of nonexistence.[67] Ill-conceived and ill-advised actions may result.

Rarely is there an attempt at deeper understanding. In addition, the public have a somewhat morbid fascination with war and violence, death and destruction. There is intense competition for dramatic images, and some in the media have been criticized for glamorizing war, with lots of pictures of soldiers in intense combat but no explanation of what is happening.[68] Pithy summaries of events, with dramatic pictures, are standard fare. The public is transfixed by tragedy. There is ample evidence of this, along with credible scientific explanations of why it occurs.[69] The news media know this and flood their outlets with images of horrific scenes, both natural and human caused. The same holds true for war coverage. There is a voyeuristic aspect to the public fascination with such images, a morbid collective interest in horror and violence.[70]

In the past, war correspondents had to file their stories in writing, first by post, then by telegraph or telephone. In the early days of television, they had to wait for ways to get films to a transmitting station. Now journalists can write stories that are published online within minutes and can be viewed globally. They are forced by the current media business models to be the first to report and to generate traffic in their stories. Obviously, none of this fosters an environment of calm, sober reflection and in-depth analysis. Much of what is written is hype, intended to inflame. Raw imagery still provides only a superficial view but often incites violence. And now some images are of highly questionable authenticity. This will be an even greater problem in the era of "deepfake" video and audio recordings, generated by artificial intelligence, that are quickly becoming so good as to be undetectable.

Nuclear weapons are considered an existential threat and to most people are terrifying. Future high-tech weapons, while not quite as frightening, are science fiction-like and mostly enigmatic to the public, giving them an aura of danger. The public are awed and transfixed by what seems to them magical: they will not try to understand the pros and cons or attempt to separate hype from reality, and they will tend to believe what the defense industry and the media tell them. While the public tend not to understand the military, they are, nonetheless, enamored with its flashy new weapons systems that are touted as game changers in the quest to make US forces more fearsome and effective. Television channels are devoted to military weapons, and movies feature such high-tech capabilities as stealth airplanes, laser weapons, and space combat. The Department of Defense and military service research labs are proud to advertise to the public the latest new weapons in an attempt to ensure future funding, and DARPA is a never-ending source of amazement for military technology junkies. The media will play on this gullibility of the public. The media love new technology. Science fiction-like stuff sells. But, as Thomas Rid warned in 2012 about the then-rapidly emerging technologies for cyber conflict, many of the new superweapons are "more hype than hazard."[71]

There is something schizophrenic about the relationship between the media and the military. The military does not really trust the media but wants to use them to advance military aims. The media do not really trust the military to be truthful and open but depend on it for information and a source of stories for the public. National leaders have historically tried to use the media to advance their own agendas, and there has long been a symbiotic relationship between the media and the military. The government of course wishes to see media products that obscure the economic and geopolitical causes of war and downplay or omit the horrors and the aftermath. Not surprisingly, the Defense Department provides support to filmmakers who depict the military in a positive light and refuses support to films deemed critical.[72] Like any large corporation, the military attempts to use the media to burnish its image, leading directly to higher recruitment rates and higher congressional appropriations. What is of concern, however, is the degree to which the military controls the narrative and the almost total lack of a counternarrative. In 1970, Senator J. William Fulbright criticized the Defense Department for promoting "a positive, yet skewed, image of war to the public."[73] Independent watchdog organizations like the Government Accountability Office (GAO) have had some limited success in highlighting military issues, but their influence is not widespread beyond a narrow group of interested parties.

Unfortunately, disinformation campaigns, which nations have employed for centuries, are made easier and far more effective by the rapid dissemination allowed by the internet and social media. Today, these platforms can be used to whip up war frenzy by rapidly disseminating conspiracy theories, to which Americans are especially susceptible. These theories, abetted by a culture with a disdain for expertise and elites and a strong cult of "common sense," result in a public in which many assert the freedom to believe things that are patently false.[74] Isaac Asimov wrote that Americans nurture the "false notion that democracy means my ignorance is just as good as your knowledge."[75] Many believe that "equal rights" means that each person's opinion about anything must be accepted as equal to anyone else's, regardless of the facts of the matter.[76] Americans have long held antipathy toward intellectuals and experts, viewing them with suspicion, resentment, and distrust.[77] Today there are far too many influential politicians and media figures who ignore, disparage, or even attempt to silence science and respected scientists.[78] Such behavior can have dangerous, even fatal, consequences when it comes to issues of public health or international conflict.

And now, there are growing examples of "conspiricism," or conspiracy theories in which there is not even an attempt at presenting facts or explanations. Events are cited that never happened, but they are reported and shared widely and quickly before they can be disproven. One disgustingly cynical example was the claim that the Sandy Hook massacre, in which twenty elementary school children and six adults were gunned down, was staged by the government. Even one of the president's multiple national security advisers claimed, without evidence, that Russian election hacking might be a false-flag operation.[79] As Jonathan Swift famously said in 1710, "Falsehood flies, and the truth comes limping after it." Sadly, his next comment is all too true: "So that when men come to be undeceived, it is too late: the jest is over; the tale has had its effect."[80] Lies and falsehoods can have real consequences. In 2016, a man entered a Washington, D.C., pizzeria and fired several shots, claiming an attempt to break up a child-trafficking ring being falsely reported by then-active conspiracy theory websites. Fortunately, no one was injured in the incident.

What is seriously concerning, however, are the national security implications of such "fake news." Consider, for example, the origins of the Spanish American War. In 1898 on the USS *Maine* in Havana Harbor, a boiler blew up, igniting the ammunition stores, and the ship sank, taking the crew down with it. While it was accidental, *the newspapers nonetheless quickly claimed that a Spanish torpedo or mine sunk the ship,* and war was then declared. In the current day, conspiracy theories abound, with assertions about "fake news' " and complaints about a vast "deep state."

Deepfakes are audio or video clips created using machine learning technology and massive data sets to, in essence, create forgeries. Simply, two AI algorithms work together, one creating the fake and one grading its efforts, with the outcome a more realistic forgery.[81] In the past, these were easily detectable by experts, but the new AI-created products are quickly becoming indistinguishable to all but the most sophisticated techniques to combat them.

Credible, but false, video, audio, or print artifacts might easily sway public opinion or worse, convince adversary military or civilian leaders that a threat was imminent, causing them to resort to unnecessary conflict. The ability to distort knowledge on a large scale could have an enormous impact. The 2019 Worldwide Threat Assessment produced by the US intelligence community warned that adversaries would probably attempt to use deepfakes or similar AI-based technologies to create convincing—but false—files to be used in influence campaigns directed against the United States and our allies.[82] Daniel Benjamin and Steven Simon were even more bold and unequivocal: "The fake news epidemic isn't just shaking up politics, it might end up causing a war, or just as consequentially, impeding a national response to a genuine threat." They continue, "Misinformation in geopolitics could lead not only to the continued weakening of our institutions but also to combat deaths."[83]

Our heavy dependence on networks and digital information is a serious but largely unresolvable vulnerability. Entities from simple hackers, to terrorist organizations, to nation-states can influence networks and information to varying degrees and with varying degrees of military or economic harm. The most insidious national threats are information operations that will cause us—either financial institutions, businesses, the military, or the public—to lose faith in our data and information and ultimately in our institutions. Cyber operations can cause, and have caused, countries and institutions to question their information and can cause supporters to lose trust. One need look no further than the 2016 US election as proof. The late Joe Hayes, a former intelligence operative and friend, wrote forcefully, "As we begin to explore the concept of trust in its many and varied dimensions in the intelligence world, we must begin from the premise that this odd world is alive with ambiguity and constant uncertainty and that complete trust may not be attainable. How do I come to trust contacts in a world of avatars?"[84]

"Imagine a society," says philosopher Sissela Bok, "no matter how ideal in other respects, where word and gesture could never be counted upon. Questions asked, answers given, information exchanged—all would be worthless. . . . Action and choice would be undermined from the outset."[85] In her 1951 book *The Origins of Totalitarianism*, philosopher Hannah Arendt, writing about Hitler's Germany in 1939, said that "the masses had reached the point where they would, at the same time, believe everything and nothing, think that everything was possible and nothing was true."[86] Arendt also worried that "the result of a consistent and total substitution of lies for factual truth is not that the lie will now be accepted as truth, and truth defamed as a lie, but that the sense by which we take our bearings in the real world . . . is being destroyed."[87]

Laboratories are racing to find ways to counter the threats from fake news and fake artifacts. Academics, decision makers, and politicians are keenly aware of the potential for incorrect or corrupted information to result in negative outcomes. Unnecessary war must top the list of those outcomes to be avoided.

THE FAILURE OF EDUCATION

Lack of education correlates strongly with militarism, nationalism, and xenophobia, a dangerous reliance on the media and on the words of politicians, and an eager acceptance of violence.

Jimmy, an anti-immigrant, hate-filled teenager from a depressed region, has lived his whole life in a rural area of shuttered businesses, crushing poverty, and marginal schools. He is bitter about his situation and the income inequality he sees and experiences every day, blaming elites, immigrants, and others for his circumstances. Jimmy is very patriotic and cannot wait to enlist in the army to fight for his country's freedoms, although he can't quite articulate just how those freedoms are being threatened beyond some vague notions about outsiders, terrorists, and Russia and China. Jimmy grew up around guns and violence in his harsh and depressing environment. He is fascinated by them and, being unemployed, spends a lot of time with military-themed video games. He finds a wealth of information and numerous like-minded individuals who agree with his intolerant, uninformed views and who argue for violent action against those he deems responsible.

Lower levels of education are characterized by a lack of skill in critical questioning and thinking, a lack of exposure to alternative viewpoints and rationale, and a lack of knowledge of other cultures and belief systems. Repeated studies have shown that less educated people tend to have more confidence in their nation's armed forces and greater preference for military action. The sociologist Seymour Martin Lipset said, "There is consistent evidence that the degree of formal education is highly correlated with undemocratic [authoritarian] attitudes."[88] Lack of exposure to history and lack of experience in complex problem-solving implies a more simplistic and less skeptical view of political leaders. This pattern is found, in varying degrees, in almost all countries. Others point out that education, in particular, has long been viewed not just as a source of higher productivity but also as crucial for developing democratic attitudes, and a substantial literature documents the inverse relationship between education and authoritarian and intolerant attitudes.[89] Jonathan Caverley provides significant evidence for a strong correlation between income inequality (as a marker for low education levels) and military aggressiveness.[90]

A more recent review of the results of forty-two studies over a twenty-year period (1996–2016) provides further definitive evidence of the correlation between better education and a lessened affinity for aggression.[91]

An extensive study was conducted in 2001 of nationalistic and xenophobic attitudes in ten countries with significant differences in citizenship and immigration regimes, from open and welcoming to tightly restrictive. Not surprisingly, levels of both sentiments diminished with increased education levels in all of the countries, *even those with restrictive policies.* The study showed clearly that education was negatively related to ethnocentrism and concluded that educational systems in all of the countries played a significant role in diminishing undemocratic and antihumanistic attitudes.[92]

Not only is there a strong correlation between poor education and authoritarian attitudes, but in the US there has long been a virulent strain of anti-intellectualism that buttresses and amplifies those attitudes. A frighteningly large number of Americans actively denigrate "too much" education and have a strong preference for "doers" over "thinkers," a situation that has repeated itself throughout history. As long ago as 472 BC, action-loving politicians in the Athenian senate argued against the diplomats, saying what far too many today seem to believe: "Lack of learning combined with sound common sense is more helpful than the kind of cleverness that gets out of hand, and . . . as a general rule states are better governed by men in the street than by intellectuals."[93]

General George C. Marshall, in his Nobel Peace Prize acceptance speech, concluded that education was an important factor affecting peace and security and suggested that schools should be more scientific and less nationalistic in teaching about the past circumstances that have led to war. Marshall wanted students to understand the conditions that had led to past tragedies, without the influence of national prejudices.[94] Such understanding can come only from the study of other nations' histories and cultures.

Nations and groups are heavily armed and growing more so, weapons are high-tech, decision-making is increasingly computer-controlled, hatred and antagonism between countries and groups are on the rise, poorly informed electorates are easily swayed, and accurate information on which to base decisions about war is increasingly rare. Everything is connected to everything else via vast networks, creating in the military something akin to a giant armed nervous system. We have, then, a recipe in which all the ingredients are there for violence to erupt. Conditions are ripe for us to stumble into war.

T H R E E

———————●———————

STUMBLING
INTO WAR

History is the unfolding of miscalculations.
—Barbara Tuchman, *Stilwell and the American Experience in China*, 1971

—————————————————————

*A friendly country experiences a devastating attack on its finan-
cial industry, creating havoc in the stock market and wiping out
the savings of tens of thousands. They say hackers stole their cyber
weapons and turned those same weapons back against them. Extremist elements in the country, however, claim that one of the
country's main adversaries is behind the financial attack. The following day, the railway system controls of the "adversary" are
hacked, derailing trains and causing head-on collisions, killing*

hundreds of passengers. While the friendly country denies any in-
volvement, claiming that the original hackers were responsible,
the adversary country's population clamors for action to be taken.
Military cyber forces of both countries call for emergency negoti-
ations, but politicians and extremist elements in both countries
clamor for war. . . .

A US satellite is conducting an inspection of an adversary nation's
satellite. The adversary country registered only one spacecraft
with the United Nations when it was launched, but ground-based
sensors have previously detected more, prompting a closer look by
the US. While conducting the sensitive rendezvous with the ad-
versary satellite—making sure to stay outside a certain safe keep-
out distance—the US satellite is struck by a high-speed object and
begins to tumble out of control and collides with the adversary
spacecraft. What is not known by either side is that a commercial
satellite that previously broke up in an intersecting orbit left pieces
that were too small to be detected but, traveling at such enormous
speeds, were enough to destroy the US inspector. The adversary
country readies its antisatellite system to destroy an equivalent
US strategic system. . . .

Too often, hotheaded leaders have used incidents and provocations as
pretexts for armed military responses. Fortunately, cooler heads have
often prevailed to keep us out of war or delay its onset. The infamous
Gulf of Tonkin incident that played such a key role in sparking the
Vietnam War stands as a perfect example of a minor incident (partly
fabricated in this case) leading to major armed conflict. In June 2019,
Iran shot down a US drone it claimed had entered its airspace in the
Strait of Hormuz. As a result, some senior US government officials ad-
vocated for military retaliation over the downing of an unarmed and
unmanned intelligence collector.[1]

The high pressure that currently pervades geopolitics, and the
presence of large numbers of both old and new weapons, combined
with an aggressive military posture and the increasingly automated
nature of command and control, can get us into a war we really do

not want. The present world situation is one in which the US, while still the global leader in technology and military strength, is being challenged on all fronts by both historic, well-armed adversaries and increasingly capable emerging nations. While military planners still concern themselves with large-scale wars pitting army against army, they now must also worry about how to employ and defend against high-tech weapons.

After the US performance in the First Gulf War, with all of its high-tech weaponry, and the later dissolution of the USSR, we spent the next decade in various adventures around the world. During this period, we were, in our own view and by all accounts, the world's only remaining superpower. We had shown the world our technological prowess with the debut of stealth airplanes, precision-guided munitions, and a highly networked intelligence, surveillance, and reconnaissance system. For a decade, we remained essentially unchallenged by peer competitor states, but with an increasing incidence of terrorism against US targets. Following the attacks of 9/11, we spent more than a decade focusing almost solely on the global war on terror. During that time, China, Russia, and others who had seen our amazing technological superiority in Kuwait and Iraq in the First Gulf War and who had seen the US use of overwhelming force in the invasion of Iraq in 2003 determined that they would not want to be dominated in such a way by the US in the future. While we chased terrorists, China and Russia aggressively modernized their military forces and equipment. Russia rearmed, China built its military, and countries like North Korea and Iran pursued nuclear weapons and ballistic missiles, while the US spent hundreds of billions of dollars and much of its energy hunting down and killing "high-value targets." Technologies on which we had started research, but which we had then put on the back burner, were high on the list of items for our competitors: hypersonics, space systems, lasers, cyber weapons, and artificial intelligence. While we were distracted, we slowly became *not* the world's only remaining superpower and began to fall behind in the technology race as well. As others were in the process of rebuilding, they were reluctant to confront the US, so no conflicts erupted. As they have gotten stronger and closer in parity, they are less intimidated, and the probability of such conflict rises.

After World War II, the US became accustomed to being the most powerful nation on earth and wielding that power around the globe. Notwithstanding the emergence of the USSR as a nuclear power, the US enjoyed an unparalleled lead for decades. This is no longer the case. We think our own superior weapons and technologies will always win the day, but this may no longer be true. While the US remains strong and powerful, other countries, especially China, are rising in stature and power, both economic and military. It is tempting to think of the US-China relationship as a new Cold War, but it differs in a fundamental way. Unlike what was the case with Russia in the Cold War, our interactions with China include deeply intertwined and interdependent economies. On the other hand, the Cold War situation with Russia, dangerous as it was, was characterized by a well-understood set of rules. The two sides actually talked and were able to manage the relationship for decades. Not only does that no longer happen, but such rules and regular military discussions do not exist with China, and the two sides must proceed cautiously with one another.[2]

Other countries in the world are now less afraid of the US and more willing to challenge it. The concern about the increased level of threatening behavior by others, combined with a perceived diminution of US influence, is that we will fall into what Harvard University professor Graham Allison termed *the Thucydides trap*.[3] His formulation of this idea argues that throughout history, whenever there has been a rapidly rising power that challenges the dominance of an existing superpower, war becomes inevitable. In the fifth century BC, Thucydides wrote that what made war inevitable was the growth of Athenian power and the fear that this caused in Sparta. Each side feared the other, and ultimately a long, brutal, disastrous war ensued. Today, we see a similar fear of China's astounding rise. Western countries, especially the US, find it hard to imagine a geopolitical order that includes an influential and technologically powerful China.[4] Unfortunately, but not surprisingly, there is increased talk in US national security circles of conflict with them. Our foreign and defense policies have become decidedly more militaristic—as have theirs. Allison makes the point that with the US and the USSR, despite moments when a violent clash seemed certain, a sense of strategic imagination—a willingness to be innovative and to challenge deep-rooted assumptions about the adversary—helped both sides develop ways to compete without a catastrophic conflict. The clear implication of his work is that such imaginative thinking does not exist today with respect to China and that the danger of war is higher as a result.

The more pertinent trap may be that decision makers' judgments in both countries will be clouded by not only fear but also hubris. The danger is that Americans' view of themselves as exceptional and entitled to a unique role in history will clash violently with an intense Chinese nationalism, with disastrous results.[5] This will be exacerbated by our unshakable, but perhaps unfounded, conviction that our weapon technologies can dominate in any conflict.

ADVERSARIES ARE TECHNOLOGY SAVVY AND WELL EQUIPPED TOO

The US, Russia, China, North Korea, and Iran—nations most often discussed—are competing on several technologies of importance to modern warfare. Clearly ballistic missiles and nuclear weapons are game changers, and while the superpowers have long held a monopoly on these, other countries seek them to gain status and to threaten their neighbors. North Korea and Iran have demonstrated remarkably rapid growth in their ballistic missile capabilities, with North Korea recently testing a missile with enough range to reach the US. All three major powers and many others are pursuing disruptive technologies, including space, cyber, artificial intelligence, and autonomous systems, and our adversaries have made great strides in these advanced technologies.

Hypersonic weapons are those that travel between five and fifteen times the speed of sound. They can be in the form of cruise missiles or maneuvering nonballistic reentry vehicles. Should they be perfected, they would be fearsome. They currently cannot be effectively defended against, and their reduced flight times will change the decision response calculus of the country targeted by them. The idea of hypersonic weapons is frightening, and their deployment would be highly destabilizing. While operationally useful hypersonic weapons are still some years away from being a reality, we and others are work-ing diligently to make them a reality.

Artificial intelligence is another enabling technology for all sorts of weapons, while obviously not itself a weapon. Partly because of the frantic writings of many scientists who understand the possibilities, the many science fiction writers who theorize about malign uses, and the companies that stand to make billions from the applications, AI has taken on the character of a possible doomsday weapon. Vladimir Putin added to the hype when he said that "the country that masters artificial intelligence will rule the world."[6] Indeed, used improperly, like any other technology, AI can be a dangerous addition to weapons arsenals.

Since the midnineties, Russia has upgraded and modernized over half of its Cold War–era military equipment. For years it used its oil wealth to fund technology investments in space, air defense, and ad-vanced technologies like cyber and AI. Russia is aggressive in its pur-suit of advanced weaponry and cyberspace capabilities and has an-nounced it is also developing autonomous underwater drones capable of carrying nuclear weapons and a nuclear-powered missile, with pre-sumably unlimited range. According to US intelligence agencies, the Russians engaged in cyber and information warfare in 2016 against the US election system.[7] In 2015, Russian hackers reportedly attacked and disabled the Ukrainian electrical grid, and in 2018 they were able to get inside the electrical power grid in the US.[8] In artificial intelli-gence, Russia is favoring military uses over commercial ones. Already, they have deployed autonomous ground systems such as tanks.[9] Cyber capabilities are, similarly, focused on military competition and a desire to frustrate US ambitions. At the strategic level, they have es-tablished a center from which to wage global information warfare.

China continues its breathtaking advances in everything from com-puter chips and genetics to hypersonics, ground-based lasers, and the broad-scale application of artificial intelligence for both civilian and military uses. It allegedly targeted US military aircraft flying near a new Chinese military base in Djibouti with advanced military-grade lasers.[10] Like Russia, it understands US vulnerabilities and is systematically striving to exploit them. China claims that its modernization is defen-sive in nature and not expansionist, while at the same time it unques-tionably uses its growing military power to exert pressure on its neighbors and to threaten US forces operating in the region. It is deploying missiles of all types at an alarming rate, and the Chinese navy is building ships, including aircraft carriers, at incredible speed. Contrasting the approaches of Russia and China, NSA cybersecurity adviser Rob Joyce has said, "We worry about Russia degrading others. China projects its power to build themselves up." He then went one better: "Russia is the hurricane, coming in fast and hard. China is climate change: long, slow, pervasive."[11] In both cases, the results can be equally damaging. China's focus on advanced technologies has an economic goal as well as a military one. The Chinese see our weak, uncoordinated attempts to secure our networks and go about stealing troves of economically and militarily important data. The US trade commissioner estimates that the annual cost of intellectual property theft is a minimum of $225 billion, with China being the principal culprit.[12] With a very long-term view, they are investing—much more than the US—in AI, cyber, genetics, quantum science, and other areas and are close to surpassing us.

Nonsuperpower countries, while they may have standing armies, have no chance of competing against the US and its heavily armed, high-tech military, so they resort to more readily available, but effective, means of attacking us. Other countries are racing to deploy drones, ballistic missiles, antiaccess technologies such as surface-to-air missiles, nuclear technologies, and cyber capabilities to challenge the great powers. Cyber techniques have grown in importance, and North Korea and Iran have successfully built capabilities. North Korea engages in theft of currency, partially to fund their weapons developments. One report alleges that North Korea illegally acquired as much as $2 billion from its increasingly sophisticated cyber activities against financial institutions and cryptocurrency exchanges.[13] Iran has an active and increasingly sophisticated cyber capability that it uses to perpetrate financial crimes as well as political interference.

Because the US military is so powerful, some of our lesser adversaries cannot or do not wish to face us in the conventional sense of war. Instead, what has emerged is so-called hybrid war or gray-zone conflict. Our adversaries use proxies and engage in forms of mischief that fall short of armed conflict. In these ways, they can destabilize a situation for the US while avoiding a direct confrontation. Techniques include crime, the sowing of political instability, cyber intrusions to disrupt facilities or to promulgate falsehoods or incite riots, sabotage, the support of mercenaries, and terror. Russian actions in Crimea and Ukraine fall into this category. That conflict has included the use of electronic warfare, cyberattacks, and drones. The new generation of technologies will be cheaper and available to more groups and even individuals. Because of the spread of these technologies, conflict may become more lawless and unpredictable.

US, Russian, and Chinese approaches to thinking about new forms of war and new technologies all focus on space and cyber dominance in some way. Russia and China believe that space is critical to "information dominance," and both seek to undermine US space-based assets with counterspace systems.[14] A recent report stated that in simulated war games against our adversaries, US communications satellites, wireless networks, and other command and control systems are heavily hacked and suppressed.[15]

China and Russia are both formidable space-faring nations. Russia's capabilities, which dropped dramatically after the fall of the USSR, have in recent years been rebuilt, with massive expenditures on military and intelligence systems and the creation of a new aerospace force. China has experienced a meteoric rise in its space capabilities, with a civil space program that aims to establish a colony on the moon in the next few years. They, too, have invested heavily in military and intelligence space systems. The US is by far the most highly dependent on space. Data from 2019 show that the US has 1,007 operational satellites, China 323, and Russia 164,[16] and Russia reports an aggressive space modernization under way.[17] Much of our military communications uses commercial satellites. Nuclear warning and command and control data is transmitted via satellite. Navigation and intelligence depend on space systems. China and Russia have consistently said that they will not allow the US to be dominant in space.[18] Sure enough, both countries have demonstrated antisatellite systems, ground and space based, to put our satellites at risk and challenge US superiority in that domain.

Threats from cyber activity and space systems are much more difficult to detect and characterize and are more likely to lead to errors in judgment. The resulting uncertainty creates a more tense global defensive posture.

While terrorist attacks remain a possibility, the danger of armed conventional attacks remains low, with the probability of an attack on the US mainland by China or Russia vanishingly small. The US enjoys a geographical buffer few countries have, with oceans on either side and friendly nations to the north and south. Nuclear attacks by either are also exceedingly improbable. While a nuclear attack by North Korea, for example, is a possibility, most experts believe that that, too, is unlikely. A far more likely scenario is for a mistake to occur in one of the hot spots around the globe where the US is being confronted and where missteps could potentially lead to a shooting war. We face adversaries and potential adversaries in Europe, Asia, Africa, the Middle East, and now potentially Latin America. In such a highly pressurized world, the chances of an accidental war are frighteningly high. The challenge is to find ways to reduce the chances of such missteps. The opportunities for miscalculation and dangerous escalation abound, however, and are abetted by the presence of new technologies.

Both Russia and China have serious disagreements with American support of countries in their regions. After the Cold War, NATO expanded to include many former Warsaw Pact countries near Russia. Poland, Hungary, and the Czech Republic joined, and then came Bulgaria, Estonia, Latvia, Lithuania, Romania, Slovakia, Slovenia, Albania, and Croatia.[19] Now NATO expansion has stopped and Russia remains in the Crimea and continues to sow discord in the border areas of Ukraine. Russia is concerned about US influence in eastern Europe and the Baltics and the stationing of US missile defense systems in closely neighboring countries. The US deploys its Aegis Ashore missile defense systems in Poland and Romania over Russian objections.[20] Russia carries out disruptive cyber influence campaigns against NATO,[21] and it is deploying robust missile systems along its western borders. The potential for a US presence in the Baltic states is a thorn in Russia's side. Russia has exerted its influence in Syria and has used that theater of operations much as the US used the First Gulf War, to showcase and test some of its advanced weapons and to demonstrate to the world its strength. Early in the Syria conflict, Russia made a public show of firing its Kalibr cruise missiles—to show the world that the US, with its Tomahawk, was not the only country capable of doing so. As we saw with the shooting down of a Russian aircraft by Turkey, Russian military forces have demonstrated aggressiveness bordering on recklessness. Provocative behavior, like that of the Russian fighter aircraft in Turkey, could result in shots being fired and could easily draw the US into conflict in support of our allies. With Crimea and Ukraine, Russia is slowly attempting to reestablish its buffer zone by annexing land around its periphery, setting up the dangerous potential for conflict with NATO. Any movement by Russia to expand its presence in Ukraine or to permanently leave troops in Belarus would be unacceptable to NATO. They have been militarily active from the Black Sea to the Baltic region, seizing Ukrainian navy vessels crossing the Kerch Strait to the Sea of Azov and deploying short-range missiles and electronic weaponry near Poland's Baltic Sea coast.[22] Additionally, Russia has actively sailed in the Arctic Sea and conducts provocative maneuvers near Norway and Denmark. An accident in Europe could easily escalate. Given its renewed aggressive military posture, Russia could mistake US and NATO intentions with military exercises as a prelude to an attack and react accordingly. This is not an idle worry. Soviet paranoia about the intentions of the US and NATO was so great in 1983 that the US Exercise Abel Archer, it has since been learned, almost resulted in a Soviet nuclear launch.[23] It remains to be seen what Russia will do in the Far East, along the border with China. The situation is fraught.

China is concerned about US influence in and military support of Taiwan, South Korea, and Japan. The US and China continue to confront one another in the South China Sea, with China building bases on artificial reefs and attempting to require countries to seek transit approval. The Chinese strategy in the western Pacific is based primarily upon long-range, land-based antiship missiles to force the US Navy to continue to operate further from their shores in wartime situations. The Chinese approach to the West seems centered on establishing Chinese regional hegemony. They of course always point to the historic ownership of Taiwan and the ultimate goal of reunification. To be sure, they could invade and occupy Taiwan, but they likely calculate that doing so would not be worth the potential cost. They have invested heavily in so-called antiaccess/area denial technologies like air and missile defenses, lasers, and jamming to preclude US access to the mainland, although it is unclear why the US would ever consider invading China or, for that matter, Russia.

The US and allies have repeatedly—and rightfully—challenged bold Chinese claims of sovereignty in the international waters of the South China Sea. This is an area where miscalculations could result in a shooting war. In conducting military exercises designed to intimidate Taiwan, China could provoke an armed response. Dangerous close approaches of aircraft and ships are all too frequent and in a heightened state of readiness create confusion and uncertainty, a situation exacerbated by the aggressive defense stance we have adopted in response. An example scenario might be one where China, rather than confront us directly, confronts one of our allies in the region, claiming a violation of territorial waters. Shots might be fired, and US vessels attempting to intervene might be accidentally struck by a Chinese antiship missile. Such accidents are far too plausible, and possible, as recently demonstrated in the Gulf of Oman when the Iranian navy mistakenly fired on one of its own ships.[24]

THE MILITARY IS ALREADY UNDER ENORMOUS STRESS

Deployed globally, heavily armed, facing adversaries in high-tension areas, and tightly connected via computers, communications, and automated systems, US forces are under enormous stress. The US military has been deployed on an average of about once per year for the last fifty years.[25] One report from the US Army Combat Studies Institute tells us that since the early 1800s, the US has engaged in less than a dozen major wars, but in several hundred other military undertakings.[26] We now have forces in a large fraction of the countries in the world. Troops are on foreign soil, aircraft carrier battle groups show up whenever there is a crisis somewhere, bombers conduct show-of-force flights, and submarines prowl the oceans. The relatively small number of combat forces is stretched thin, given the number of missions they are asked to perform.

Many soldiers have deployed to combat zones multiple times. Air force aircraft are wearing out rapidly, with close to 30 percent being not combat-ready because of maintenance and parts issues. In the bomber fleet, the availability of some systems is at 50 percent.[27] Navy personnel are deployed as frequently as the army and have little time to train. A recent series of fatal ship accidents was attributed in part to sailor fatigue and lack of time for training. For example, Vice Admiral Joseph Aucoin was alarmed and angered by what he found with the Seventh Fleet during his time as the commander, writing: "The fleet was short of sailors, and those it had were often poorly trained and worked to exhaustion. Its warships were falling apart, and a bruising, ceaseless pace of operations meant there was little chance to get necessary repairs done. The very top of the Navy was consumed with buying new, more sophisticated ships."[28] Aucoin repeatedly raised the alarm to navy leaders, warning them that the bruising pace of operations could not be safely sustained. Former secretary of defense James Mattis told Congress that "the longest continued period of combat in our nation's history created an *overstretched and under-resourced* military."[29] Even with enormous military budgets, we are getting too few highly expensive weapons systems and investing too little in people and the things needed to support the systems we get.

In a related development, the US Navy is modifying its fleet of guided-missile destroyers to revert back to old technology after a series of incidents, including a collision, convinced commanders that the complexity of the system, combined with inadequate time for training, was overwhelming the operators. Sailors in the fleet preferred mechanical controls and a physical throttle over the complex touchscreen system at the helm.[30] The navy's experience should serve as a caution against the continued rush to put complex, high-tech weapons into operations. Soldiers and sailors should not have to struggle with complex interfaces between themselves and their equipment. In this case, the technology developers were in the wrong, prioritizing system efficiency over usability in combat.

Nonstop deployments are taking an enormous toll on our soldiers, sailors, airmen, and marines. Our special operations forces, in particular, are being stretched to the breaking point. The tempo of operations and the lack of downtime increase the incidence of mistakes, some deadly. Former commander of special operations forces Admiral William McRaven said several years ago, "My soldiers have been fighting now for 12, 13 years in hard combat. And anybody that has spent any time in this war has been changed by it. It's that simple."[31]

THREATS

Threats of new enemy capabilities and threats of war often act like self-fulfilling prophecies. They involve mass psychology and create a form of hysteria that then further promotes the risk of war.[32] We saw this, of course, in the run-up to the war in Iraq in 2003, with repeated warnings of weapons of mass destruction that were never found and likely never existed.

Over the last few years, the number of threats issued by the political leaders of key countries has increased. The use of competitive and even aggressive language in military and foreign affairs has become more common, with a 10 percent increase in the number of instances between January 2015 and September 2018—most of that occurring after July 2017.[33] There have been exchanges of threats between the US and Russia, between the US and North Korea, and between the US and Iran, some of them involving nuclear weapons.[34]

Rational actors—most countries, but not terror groups—really do not want armed conflict but use threats of it to sway the decision-making of their adversaries. Often, threatening and boasting behavior on the part of a leader is as much for domestic consumption as anything else.[35] What we now see as threats are mostly warmongering and posturing. However, when leaders begin to actually believe their own propaganda, and when the boasting and bragging are backed up by actions, the situation becomes more dangerous. Leaders succumb to hubris; they believe in the war-winning capability of their unstoppable weapons and the inevitability of their success. They act according to their wishes, undeterred by facts, with what Barbara Tuchman calls "wooden-headedness."[36]

It is important not to confuse capabilities with threats. The definition of a threat includes *both capability and intent*. A threat is a threat only if the owner of a capability intends to use it. If the intent is not known, only the capability exists, and thus the threat is just a perception. The US all too often overreacts to adversary technical capabilities, depicting them as imminent threats, when, in fact, other countries are only seeking to achieve capabilities that the US already has.

AN INCREASED AGGRESSIVENESS

"Never has our future been more unpredictable, never have we depended so much on political forces that cannot be trusted to follow the rules of common sense and self-interest—forces that look like sheer insanity, if judged by the standards of other centuries."[37] These words from Hannah Arendt in 1950 read as if they could have been written today. She goes on to say that desperate hope and desperate fear seem to define events more than balanced judgment and measured insight—again, a good description of our current state of world affairs.

The national security strategy of the US was, until recently, aimed at building relations with allies and adversaries and attempting to dampen tensions, while maintaining a robust military capability. The current strategy is far more warlike in its tone. It has taken a clear and disturbing turn toward more aggressiveness and bellicosity and says nothing about reducing deployments and the burden on an already highly stretched military. Our policies have gone from necessary preparedness and cooperation to threat and provocation. The strategy makes clear that we have moved from fighting terror as our main concern to facing peer nations like Russia and China in a return of great power competition and that the only way to respond is through more power and better weapons. This is now the primary concern in US national security. As the 2018 National Defense Strategy Summary put it, "The central challenge to US prosperity and security is the reemergence of long-term, strategic competition," concluding, "It is increasingly clear that China and Russia want to shape a world consistent with their authoritarian model."[38]

The past few years have seen massive increases in funding for new war-fighting technologies and new weapons. The strategic approach calls for more spending on weapons and advanced technologies like space, hypersonics, cyber, and artificial intelligence, with the Defense

Department saying in 2018 that "a more lethal, resilient, and rapidly innovating Joint Force will sustain American influence and ensure favorable balances of power."[39] Unfortunately, the strategy documents were weak or silent on other national security issues like climate change, arms proliferation, and pandemic diseases, none of which can be solved by buying more weapons.[40]

The 2018 strategy put far more emphasis on competition and conflict than do those of 2008 and 2015. The 2008 strategy expressed a goal of building collaborative and cooperative relationships with Russia and China. In 2015, even after provocative actions by China in the South China Sea and Russia in the Crimea, the US was still committed to substantial military-to-military relationships and engagement. By 2018, the tone and content had changed dramatically.[41] The current strategy pursues military power as an end in itself, with the notion that a more militaristic approach to American foreign policy improves our relative power position—hard power being the key concept. Absent from our approach is any hint of so-called soft power, "the cultural, ideological, and institutional tools to bring other countries in line with US ideals."[42] Naturally, our change in approach to foreign policy has been mirrored by that of our competitors. The phrase "preparation for military struggle" now appears in the most recent Chinese strategy but was barely mentioned in their documents in 2008 and 2010. Russia now perceives a competitive and hostile security environment and identifies increasing global competition as a military threat.[43] It remains to be seen how, or if, the new administration will alter the approach to the tense national security situations around the globe.

Current cyber and space strategies naturally reflect the increased aggressiveness. New strategies talk about "active defense" and "defending forward," which essentially mean that if we are the subject of adversary actions we deem damaging or threatening, we will reach out to neutralize those threats. Cyber experts assure us that we will limit our actions to eliminating the immediate threat and will not pursue so-called offensive actions. However, because cyber operations are so nearly instantaneous, preemptive attack becomes an appealing option. This sounds dangerously close to the idea of preemptive nuclear attack, in which the country uses its weapons rather than risk losing them. As Thomas Schelling said in describing nuclear weapons strategy, "If the weapons can act instantaneously by the flip of a switch, and can arrive virtually without warning to do decisive damage, the outcome of the crisis depends simply on who first finds the suspense unbearable."[44]

One noteworthy development is that in the 2019 National Defense Authorization Act, the law now grants authority to launch an offensive cyberattack to military commanders, an authority that previously was held at the National Command Authority (NCA) level, demonstrating once again an increased willingness and readiness to actually engage in conflict.[45] One legal analyst calls the change a "preauthorization to use military force."[46] While from a warfighter's perspective it makes some sense to give commanders tactical flexibility, it worryingly increases the number of individuals who can initiate a cyber conflict—and thus the number of individual opinions about what constitutes adequate rationale for doing so. We should also consider that there are many who think of and refer to cyber weapons as "weapons of mass destruction."[47] Russia has argued at the United Nations that the potential destructiveness of cyber weapons could rival that of nuclear weapons.[48] Like our national cyber strategy, the strategy of Russia, for instance, reserves for them the right to respond to a cyberattack with any weapon of their choosing up to, and including nuclear weapons. Is that a decision we want to be allowed below the level of the national leadership?

While we may have thought that the era of a nuclear arms race had ended, Russia has developed and maintains tactical, low-yield, nuclear weapons that they claim will be used if they are ever invaded. With little understandable rationale beyond the fact that Russia has them and we do not, the previous president called for new tactical nuclear systems for the US. In a syntactical and logical puzzle, the 2018 Nuclear Posture Review (NPR) stated that "expanding flexible U.S. nuclear options now, to include low-yield options, is important for the preservation of credible deterrence against regional aggression. To be clear, this is not intended to enable, nor does it enable, 'nuclear warfighting.' Nor will it lower the nuclear threshold. Rather, expanding U.S. tailored response options will raise the nuclear threshold and help ensure that potential adversaries perceive no possible advantage in limited nuclear escalation, making nuclear weapons employment less likely."[49]

There is dangerous talk of launching space-based weapons—accompanied by the recent establishment of the US Space Force (USSF), which lists as one of its missions the preparation for war in space. New space force doctrine calls for the development of "combat-ready" space forces and includes such topics as *orbital warfare* and space *battle management*. Other countries are very concerned about US moves to station interceptors in space as an element of our missile defense forces and view such talk as provocative and destabilizing.[50]

With such an aggressive strategy, it is only a matter of time before soldiers and officers at the small unit level on the front lines begin to translate that new aggressive stance not only into military planning but also into daily behavior. This has, in fact, already begun. Overeager space operators, emboldened by the successful stand-up of the new Space Force, gleefully give interviews in which they discuss preparing for war in space. Even the secretary of the air force, addressing a large symposium of space industry executives, says it may be time for the US to conduct a show of force in space just to put our adversaries on notice.[51] Really? Do we really think it necessary to be this provocative, and do we really think the benefits outweigh the dangers?

Although it was decades ago, I myself have been party to what, in hindsight, seem dangerous and petty provocations that could have ended very badly. In the late 1970s, I was assigned as a platoon leader in a mechanized infantry brigade whose mission was to position itself astride the Fulda Gap in Germany, where it would be one of the first in combat against the Warsaw Pact forces anticipated to overrun western Europe. Regularly we stood watch over our portion of the East German border, in clear sight of booby-trapped fences and heavily armed guard towers. Just for fun, we would watch gleefully as our hot-shot pilots would often come flying in at low level and high speed directly at the East German guard towers and, at the last minute, turn sharply away. Dutifully, the border guards would raise and train their automatic weapons on the aircraft, ready to shoot them down. To my knowledge no violence ever erupted, but our fun was exceedingly foolhardy. Later, I was assigned to a unit that stored and maintained tactical

nuclear weapons. At the time both the US and the USSR main-
tained "liaison missions" that were authorized to travel freely
around adversary territory to view military movements—except
in specified cases, one of these being nuclear weapons facilities.
Frequently, the Soviet Military Liaison Mission would come re-
gardless, and we just as frequently would chase them away. It was
all part of a day's work. In March 1985, an American army major,
conducting a surveillance mission in East Germany, allegedly got
too close to a secure, restricted installation and was shot and killed
by guards. The point of all this is that provocative behavior is for
the most part unnecessary and its potential downsides are huge.

It remains to be seen how the national strategy and military strategy approaches will translate to rules of engagement for deployed forces and actual behavior. However, over time, the aggressive posture of the president and his national security team is translated into the combatant commander's guidance and seeps into the psyches of the soldiers on the front lines. The US Army describes the *commander's intent* as "a succinct description of what constitutes success for the operation, including the purpose, key tasks, and the *conditions that define the end state* [italics mine]. A clear commander's intent facilitates a shared understanding."[52] If at every level of the chain of command, beginning with the commander in chief, the approach to adversaries is belligerent, that mode of behavior will replicate itself among lower-level troops who wish to follow their commander's lead. If the top-level strategy calls for forces to "defend forward," then troops on the front lines will adopt that mindset as well.

DANGERS OF RAMPANT MILITARISM

I served in the military in the decades spanning the end of the Vietnam War to the post-9/11 invasion of Iraq and the war on terror. In that time, I watched and participated as the military went from being widely mistrusted to being the subject of veneration by the public. Neither extreme is good or healthy. After Vietnam, military leaders worked to reestablish trust and competency and over the next decade largely succeeded. The Reagan buildup of the late 1980s further cemented the redemption. The fall of the USSR and the victory of the US in the First Gulf War demonstrated just how far we had come. America's dominant technological prowess was on full display, and over the next decade the US military was everywhere. The attacks of 9/11 and the subsequent invasions of Afghanistan and Iraq, followed by the long war on terror, ensured that the military would continue to demand the public's respect and attention. What I have seen is an attitude toward the military that has evolved from public derision to grudging respect, to an unhealthy, unquestioning veneration. Polls repeatedly list the military as one of the most respected institutions in the country, and deservedly so. The object of that adulation, *the military*, is one thing, but *militarism* is something else entirely and is something about which the public should be concerned. As a nation, we have become alarmingly militaristic. Every international problem is looked at first through a military lens; then maybe diplomacy will be considered as an afterthought. Non-military issues as diverse as budget deficits and demographic trends are now called national security issues. Soldiers, sailors, airmen, and marines are all now referred to as "warfighters," even those who sit behind a desk or operate satellites thousands of miles in space. We are endlessly talking about threats and dismiss those who disagree or dissent as weak, or worse, unpatriotic.

The young men and women who serve deserve our greatest regard and the best equipment the US has to offer. Part of the respect we could show them, however, is to attempt to understand more about them and to question the mindset that is so eager to employ them in conflicts. In the words of a soldier frequently deployed to war zones in Iraq and Afghanistan, "[An] important question is how nearly two decades of sustained combat operations have changed how the Army sees itself. . . . I feel at times that the Army culturally defines itself less by the service it provides and more by the wars it fights. This observation may seem silly at first glance. After all, the Army exists to fight wars. Yet a soldier's sense of identity seems increasingly tied to war, not the service war is supposed to provide to our nation."[53]

A 1955 American Friends Service Committee pamphlet titled *Speak Truth to Power* described eloquently the effects of American fascination with militarism:

The open-ended nature of the commitment to militarization prevents the pursuit of alternative diplomatic, economic, and social policies that are needed to prevent war. The constant preparation for war and large-scale investment in military readiness impose huge burdens on society, diverting economic, political and psychological resources to destructive purposes. Militarization has a corrosive effect on social values . . . distorting political culture and creating demands for loyalty and conformity. . . . Under these conditions, mass opinion is easily manipulated to fan the flames of nationalism and military jingoism.[54]

Barbara Tuchman described the national situation with regard to the Vietnam War in a way eerily similar to the present. First was an overreaction and overuse of the term *national security* and the conjuring up of specters and visions of ruin if we failed to meet the imagined threat. Second was the "illusion" of omnipotence and the failure to understand that conflicts were not always soluble by the application of American force. Third was an attitude of "Don't confuse me with the facts": a refusal to credit evidence in decision-making. Finally—and perhaps most importantly in today's situation—was "a total absence of reflective thought" about what we were doing. Political leaders embraced military action on the basis of a perceived, but largely uninformed, view of our technological and military superiority. The public, unwilling to make the effort to challenge such thinking, just went along. "There is something in modern political and bureaucratic life," Tuchman concluded, "that subdues the functioning of the intellect."[55]

HIGH TECH COULD MAKE MISTAKES MORE LIKELY

Almost the entire world is connected and uses computer networks, but we're never really sure whether they are secure or whether the information they carry is truthful. Other countries are launching satellites, outer space is getting very crowded, and there is increased talk of competition and conflict in space. Countries engage in attacks on adversary computers and networks, and militaries are rediscovering the utility of electronic warfare, employing radio-frequency (RF) signals to damage, disrupt, or spoof other systems. While in cyber war and electronic warfare the focus is on speed, they and space conflict are characterized by significant ambiguity. Cyber incidents and space incidents as described earlier, characterized as they are by such great uncertainty, give the hotheads ample reason to call for response, and the cooler heads reasons to question the wisdom of such a move.

What could drag us into conflict? Beyond the geographical hot spots, a mistake or miscalculation in the ongoing probes of each other's computer networks could trigger an unwanted response. US weapon systems are extremely vulnerable to such probes. A 2018 study by the Government Accountability Office found mission-critical vulnerabilities in systems, and testers were able to take control of systems largely undetected. Worse yet, government managers chose not to accept the seriousness of the situation.[56] A cyber probe of our infrastructure could be mistaken for an attack and result in retaliation, setting off response and counterresponse, escalating in severity, and perhaps lethality. Much of the DOD's high-priority traffic uses space systems that are vulnerable to intrusion and interference from an increasing number of countries. Electronic warfare against military radios and radars is a growing concern as these capabilities improve.

China and Russia both have substantial space programs, and they intend to challenge the US in space, where we are vulnerable. With both low-earth and geosynchronous orbits becoming increasingly crowded, and with adversary countries engaging in close approaches to our satellites, the situation is ripe for misperception. What is mere intelligence gathering could be misconstrued as an attack and could generate a response, either in space or on the ground. There could be attacks, both direct and surreptitious, on our space systems. Or there could be misunderstandings, with too-close approaches of other satellites viewed as threatening. Threats could be space-based or, more likely, ground-based interference, jamming, or dazzling by lasers. Commercial satellite imagery recently revealed the presence of an alleged ground-based laser site in China, presumed by intelligence analysts to be for attacks against US satellites. Russia has engaged in close, on-orbit station-keeping with high-value US systems.[57] New technology weapons give their owners a new sense of invincibility, and an action that might have in the past been considered too dangerous or provocative might now be deemed worth the risk.

Enormous vulnerability comes along with the high US dependence on networks. As the scenarios at the beginning of this chapter suggest, in a highly charged atmosphere, the uncertainty and ambiguity surrounding incidents involving some of the new war-fighting technologies can easily lead to misperceptions and, ultimately, violence. The battlefield is chaotic, uncertain, and unpredictable anyway. Such technological additions—and the vulnerabilities they entail—only make it more so. A former UK spy chief has said, "Because technology has allowed humans to connect, interact, and share information almost instantaneously anywhere in the world, this has opened channels where misinformation, blurred lines, and ambiguity reign supreme."[58]

It is easy to see how such an ambiguous environment could make a soldier or military unit anxious to the point of aggression. To carry the "giant armed nervous system" metaphor a bit further, consider a human being who is excessively "nervous." Psychologists and neuroscientists tell us that excessive aggression and violence likely develop as a consequence of generally disturbed emotional regulation, *such as abnormally high levels of anxiety*.[59] Under pressure, an individual is unlikely to exhibit what we could consider rational behavior. Just as a human can become nervous, supersensitive, overly reactive, jumpy, perhaps "trigger-happy," so too can the military. A military situation in which threats and uncertainty abound will probably make the forces anxious or "nervous." Dealing with ambiguity is stressful. Some humans are able to deal successfully with such ambiguity. The ability of machines to do so is an open question.

Technologies are not perfect, especially those that depend on thousands or millions of lines of software code. A computer or human error by one country could trigger a reaction by another. A computer exploit intended to gather intelligence or steal data might unexpectedly disrupt a critical part of an electric grid, a flight control system, or a financial system and end up provoking a nonproportional and perhaps catastrophic response. The hyperconnectedness of people and systems, and the almost-total dependence on information and data, are making the world—and military operations—vastly more complicated. Some military scholars are concerned about emerging technologies and the possibility of unintended, and uncontrollable, conflict brought on by decisions made by autonomous systems and the unexpected interactions of complex networks of systems that we do not fully understand. Do the intimate connections and rapid communication of information make a "knee-jerk" reaction more, or less, likely? Does the design for speed and automation allow for rational assessment, or will it ensure that a threat impulse is matched by an immediate, unfiltered response? Command and control can, and sometimes does, break down when the speed of operations is so great that a commander feels compelled to act immediately, even if he or she does not really understand what is happening. If we do not completely understand the systems—how they are built, how they operate, how they fail—they and we could make bad and dangerous decisions.

Technological systems, if they are not well understood by their operators, can cascade out of control. The horrific events at Chernobyl are sufficient evidence of that. Flawed reactor design and inadequately trained personnel, with little understanding of the concept of operation, led to a fatal series of missteps. Regarding war, Richard Danzig points to the start of World War I.[60] The antagonists in that war had a host of new technologies never before used together on such a scale: railroads, telegraphs, the bureaucracy of mass mobilization, quick-firing artillery, and machine guns. The potential to deploy huge armies in a hurry put pressure on decision makers to strike first before the adversary was ready, employing technologies they really didn't understand. Modern technology can create the same pressure for a first strike that the technology of 1914 did. Americans are especially impatient. Today, computer networks, satellites in orbit, and other modern infrastructures are relatively fragile, giving a strong advantage to whichever side strikes first. Oxford professor Lucas Kello notes that "in our era of rapid technological change, threats and opportunities arising from a new class of weapons produce pressure to act before the laborious process of strategic adoption concludes."[61] In other words, we rush them to the field before we have done the fundamental work of figuring out their proper use.

Decorated Vietnam veteran Hal Moore described the intense combat on the front lines with his soldiers in the Ia Drang campaign in 1965.[62] He told, in sometimes gruesome detail, of the push and shove of the battle and how he would, from time to time, step back slightly to gather his thoughts and *reflect* on what was happening and, just as importantly, what was not happening. Political leaders, overwhelmed by pressures of too much information and too little time, are deprived of the ability to think or reflect on the context of a situation.[63] They are hostage to time and do not have the luxury of what philosopher Simone Weil calls "between the impulse and the act, the tiny interval that is reflection."[64]

Today's battles, which will probably happen at lightning speed, may not allow such a luxury as reflection. Hypersonic missiles, for instance, give their targets precious little time for decision-making and might force ill-informed and ill-advised counterdecisions.[65] Autonomous systems, operating individually or in swarms, connected via the internet in a network of systems, create an efficient weapon system. A mistake by one, however, could speed through the system with possibly catastrophic consequences.[66] The digital world's emphasis on speed further inhibits reflection.

With systems so far-flung, so automated, and so predisposed to action, it will be essential to find ways to program our weapon systems to prevent unrestrained independent, autonomous aggression. However, an equally, if not more, important goal will be to identify ways to inhibit not only the technology but also the decision makers' proclivity to resort to violence.

F O U R

AVOIDING WAR

It would be better for our country and the world in general,
if at least the few people who were capable of thought
stood for reason and the love of peace instead
of heading wildly with blind obsession for new war.
—Herman Hesse, *Steppenwolf*

In the aftermath of World War II and with the start of the Cold War, citizens worried about, and experienced an existential dread of, thermonuclear Armageddon. While the Cold War per se has ended and the numbers of weapons have been reduced dramatically in the US and Russia, nuclear technologies continue to proliferate around the world. Some senior officials say that it is not a matter of "if" a nuclear event will occur, only a matter of "when."[1] From the end of World War II to 1973, the US was involved in 19 military operations. From 1973 to

2012, there were 144.[2] The US has conducted more armed interventions since the end of the Cold War than during it.[3] At some level, everyone agrees that war and violence are bad things, but we keep engaging in them.

We have to ask ourselves several important questions. How did things get this way? Citizens cede war-making authority and responsibility to political leaders, who then freely engage us in conflicts that we do not understand and that often have little to do with our own security. Worse yet, we repeatedly let them do so with little, or no, pushback. When and why did citizens become so detached from America's wars? The public pays little attention. It is not directly affected. Why should the public even care? At some point, the costs—personal, financial, reputational—of US involvement in endless wars will have to be paid. What information should citizens have and should they demand if the politicians decide to deploy troops? They will need to be informed if they are to push back against the undebated policies and the unrestrained behavior of politicians in using military force. What role do new war-fighting technologies play in these decisions, if at all? With new weapons technologies, there will be new and different pressures, which makes the search for ways to avoid war even more important. These all add up to the fundamental questions of why and how people should resist war in this era of new technologies and new types of conflict.

HOW DID THINGS GET THIS WAY?

How did we get to the point where national leaders view almost all issues of foreign affairs through the lens of military action? The behavior of US leaders has long been such that when faced with a difficult foreign policy situation, they freely opt to use military might rather than diplomacy to implement their views of how it should be resolved. Senator J. William Fulbright, a fierce critic of America's repeated resort to military solutions, spoke in 1966 of our unmatched military power infecting our thinking and leading us to imperialist attitudes and war-like behavior. Fulbright decried the arrogance of our foreign policies, noting that our history of intolerant Puritanism often led us "to look at the world through the distorting prism of a harsh and angry moralism." "Power," he said, "has a way of planting delusions of grandeur in the minds of otherwise sensible people."[4] Some scholars have concluded that during the nineteenth and twentieth centuries the United States was by far the most violent of its peer group of nations. This has continued unabated into the twenty-first century, with numerous American military interventions, or the threat of them, around the globe. To one European observer, we stand out as obsessed with the symbolic importance of war and violence.[5] There are far too many who tout "American exceptionalism" and our special role in the world. The US is indeed an exceptional nation in a host of ways, but they believe that we are somehow *more* upstanding, moral, and noble than other countries and that our values and culture are simply superior to those of other nations. They expect others to submit to our leadership because of what we feel is its self-evident goodness, and we resort to force when they do not. One writer called this "a particularly arrogant brand of exceptionalism."[6]

Americans have become complacent about war, especially since the advent of the all-volunteer military. They are not directly involved, they do not seem to realize that they are actually paying dearly for our endless wars, and they are consumed by other quotidian interests. Americans have no true sense of war's awful costs. The vast majority of citizens are ill informed on—and even less interested in learning about—military issues, including the reasons why our military is so frequently used. They are overcome by inertia. Either it is not a problem for them at all or it is one over which they can have no influence. So they do nothing.

WAR HAS BECOME TOO EASY

Americans have been lulled into thinking war will be easy. Long-range weapons and airpower and a protracted fight with less capable enemies have made it look as if we can always win with minimal effort. And, of course, we think that with all of our powerful new weapons, we will always prevail.

Over time, the weapons of war have allowed humans to fight at increasingly greater distances. From the sticks and clubs of early man to pikes, to longbows, to artillery, to ballistic missiles and cruise missiles, to lasers, to high-speed global strike weapons, humans have been able to kill farther and farther from the battlefield. Technological innovations in weapons fundamentally change the nature of war, and while new technologies like cyber weapons and autonomous systems promise to further reduce risk to soldiers, they will make it far too easy to resort to the use of force. Because soldiers will be at lower risk of becoming casualties, the psychological barrier and the costs of entry to violence are lowered, and along with them any hesitation about the use of military force. As I have written, "On battlefields of the future, technology will deaden our senses to the horror of war and its consequences."[7] In accepting the 2002 Nobel Peace Prize, former president Jimmy Carter said that "in order for us human beings to commit ourselves personally to the inhumanity of war, we find it necessary to first dehumanize our opponents. . . . From a great distance, we launch bombs or missiles with almost total impunity and never want to know the number or identity of the victims."[8] How are we to resist this tendency? We must be reminded and understand that, while these systems make going to war easy, once war is started, the complex and often messy tasks of ending the war and planning the peace begin. At its core, war is about imposing one's will on the adversary. Once the bombing and missile strikes are done, soldiers must ultimately become involved.

New high-tech weapons are so good and so accurate that planners will find it difficult to resist the urge to use them. That being the case, the criteria for using them may be relaxed.[9] Technology makes different kinds of low-level conflict far too easy and tempts military planners into thinking that will always be true. In addition, many of these new technologies are far cheaper than the conventional weapons of the past, which makes them more affordable to use more frequently. The availability of such weapons will allow the decision makers to wage wars without, at least initially, committing troops. We can fire Tomahawk missiles from the Mediterranean Sea into Al Qaeda training camps or at Syrian targets. Israel can attack Syrian nuclear facilities with cyber weapons and bombs. Presumably, we can destroy Iranian centrifuges with cyber weapons. Targeted drone strikes can be directed from bases in Nevada. Soon, we will be able to send high-speed missiles toward targets around the world in just over an hour.

According to the true technology zealots and proselytizers, war promises to be clean, antiseptic, easy, run by computers, and fought from afar. It will be said that US technology is the best in the world and that we have technology countermeasures for whatever the enemy uses to confront us. With the new generation of weapons technologies, war will be fought at a distance, at frightening speeds, and presumably with overwhelming superiority, employing stealth, long-range cruise missiles, high-powered electromagnetic weapons, lasers, and other (less messy) nonconventional means. Conflicts may begin with technology such as missile strikes, bombing, and cyberattacks, but planners must then answer the question: Now what?

COMPLACENCY, INERTIA

At the level of military operations, average citizens have little power to affect the proclivity to war. They can force politicians to act, or not act, by asking probing questions and letting their representatives know how they feel, but such active involvement is rare. Unfortunately, the American public displays little interest and a lot of apathy about issues of military and foreign affairs. As writer Andrew Bacevich put it, "A collective indifference to war has become an emblem of contemporary America."[10] Novelist Ann Bridges adds even more scathingly that "we are talking about an America singularly lacking in intellectual curiosity and its citizens' will to study, consider, debate, and actively choose what both the purpose and nature of future conflicts should be."[11] This complacency might be attributed to forms of inertia plaguing individual citizens. In the first case, citizens see the problems of foreign affairs and war as too difficult and just give up, allowing the politicians to call the shots as they see fit. They feel that democracy has failed them and that they have little influence on the behavior of their elected representatives anyway. In the second, equally worrying, case, they think all the anxiety and hand-wringing is merely overblown.[12] In one view of the reaction to serious world events, Americans think things are so bad that nothing can be done. In another view, they believe that somehow all will be well and they go on about their daily routines unfazed. In either case, the result is the same.[13]

Why are they so seemingly uninterested? Average citizens have no stake or interest: they do not pay—not directly anyway—for the wars we fight, nor are they asked to participate. In general, Americans and their counterparts in other Western countries are just too self-absorbed to care. As journalist David Brooks has noted, "Our problem is that most people are entirely disengaged from great public matters. Consumed by private pleasures, they almost never invest their passions in dreams of a better world."[14] For average citizens, war is something "over there." It is, for them, risk-free and very easy to start. By relying on proxies to fight for us, and by depending so heavily on secretive special operations forces and airpower, military operations barely make it into Americans' consciousness, if at all. Today, more than ever, citizens are overwhelmed with data and information, and in the ongoing battle for their attention, topics like immigration, health care, domestic political standoffs, and, of course, the travails of the latest hot entertainer or sports figure, are front and center. Issues of foreign policy and the military lose the battle for the public's already woefully limited attention span. Even when soldiers are killed or wounded and the media report it, the reactions are fleeting. How many news cycles did the Iranian rocket attack on an overseas base housing US troops last? Not many. The apathy Americans demonstrate about our wars is astounding.[15]

The detachment many Americans feel concerning America's wars is due in some measure to those wars' relative invisibility. At various times in the past, the government has sought to limit public knowledge of our involvement in wars. The first Bush administration instituted a long-running policy of forbidding photographs of coffins arriving in the US of soldiers killed in combat. In the Gulf War, reporters were "embedded" with military units and were often allowed access to only uninteresting and uncontroversial information. Contrast this with media coverage of the Vietnam War. It is widely, but not universally, believed that video footage from reporters, especially after the 1968 Tet Offensive, turned the tide of American public opinion against the war.[16] Today, the administration has heavily restricted information on troop deployments that was previously made public, citing reasons of operational security. Much of what the military does is hidden from view of the average citizen, either because it is just not advertised or because it is expressly kept secret. What do citizens have a right to know, and what should be kept secret? The public has a right to know what military operations we are involved in, and why. It is not necessary that they know all the operational details that, by necessity, must remain secret to protect our forces.

In something of a "catch-22," the president can and does deploy troops freely, after which he notifies members of Congress, who are then unwilling to question the action or interfere with the commander in chief while the country is "at war." The president, when pushed, announces a troop deployment with vague comments about how it ensures our continued way of life and protects the safety and security of Americans, without ever explaining to a gullible citizenry why that is so. How do we let this happen? Once we are in a conflict, the public rightfully wishes the best for troops fighting the battles and is loath to criticize the war, lest they appear unpatriotic or, worse, that they might affect the morale and safety of those in combat. They somehow do not make the crucial distinction: criticizing or questioning the decision to go to war in no way criticizes those being ordered to engage in it. It could be argued, in fact, that not asking political leaders to justify their decisions is an even more egregious affront to our troops. In 1946, the historian and philosopher Lewis Mumford wrote about our political leaders as "madmen," who were convinced they were working for peace while engaging in war preparations.[17] Obviously, he concluded, we must be madmen too if we so willingly acquiesced in such behavior. The situation brings to mind the frequently used, though not entirely accurate, depiction of lemmings following one another over a cliff in an unthinking act of mass suicide.

WHY SHOULD THE PUBLIC EVEN CARE?

The American public seems fairly blasé about our frequent military deployments. Only after we are technologically involved does the requirement to deploy boots on the ground become apparent, and even then, it is often accomplished by sending special operations forces on missions that the public never sees. Too often we get into conflicts first and then the public and Congress react. We must find a way to prevent this. Given the American history of militarism and our being anxious to go to war but quickly tiring of it, promises of quick victory are inviting. Unfortunately, memories are short and the results will probably be the same as before. Recall 2003's "shock and awe," in which our overwhelming firepower and advanced systems were to make short work of the US invasion of Iraq. It did not quite work out that way.

There are numerous examples of technology being touted as a way to shorten or end wars and just the opposite happening. The well-known cases of Alfred Nobel and Richard Gatling stand as perfect examples. Nobel thought that the mutual annihilation enabled by dynamite from his factories would cause civilized nations to recoil with horror and disband their troops.[18] Gatling thought his machine gun would be a means of shortening wars, not making them more horrific.[19] Later in history, US air forces in World War II were sure that so-called strategic bombing, the deliberate targeting of civilian population centers with high explosives and incendiary bombs, would bring the enemy to the bargaining table. Just the opposite was true; it strengthened their resolve. In Vietnam, the US employed all of its modern weaponry, including helicopters, millions of pounds of bombs, and millions of gallons of defoliants, against an "inferior" enemy but lost the war anyway and in the process created an environmental nightmare in that country.

From gunpowder to strategic bombing, to the so-called revolution in military affairs, a technological superiority that was to have given the US unassailable military prowess, things have also not necessarily always turned out as expected. In his 2003 Army War College paper "Crack in the Foundation," then lieutenant colonel H. R. McMaster wrote that the intellectual foundation of future military force was based on the idea that emerging and rapidly growing information technologies would permit US forces to achieve a very high degree of certainty in future military operations. Military planners further assumed that with dominant information superiority and the resulting battlespace knowledge, commanders could predict, with very high confidence, near-term enemy actions and combat outcomes. New theories of war took on names evoking a sense of control.[20] Such terms as *network centric warfare* and *information age war* placed decision-making in the realm of advanced networks and computing and downplayed the importance of the human. Command and control was grounded in the assumption that technology would provide near certainty. It would, as Admiral Bill Owens wrote at the time, "lift the fog of war."[21] Near-perfect information was to make possible precise application of force from great distances, which would, in turn, reduce the risk to US forces and minimize "collateral damage." Almost two decades later the arguments, and promises, are the same. Now technology advocates again point to advances in weapons and artificial intelligence as revolutionary and game-changing. It isn't clear the results will be any different.

It seems that, in the current era, the American public will take an interest and become involved in military or foreign affairs only when a situation directly involves them. Unlike Russia or China, where borders and wars have defined their long histories, the US mainland has never been attacked in the traditional military sense. They, in contrast, have experienced numerous invasions, and there is a wide realization and understanding of military and security issues among their citizenry.[22] In an astounding comment, one college student, when I asked what would make her worry about nuclear war, replied that she would be concerned if one were used in an attack—in the US. Apparently, nuclear conflict elsewhere was unimportant. With the demise of conscripted military service and the growth of the professional military in the US, the individual citizen has no stake, and therefore little interest, in military operations. Such deliberate ignorance of such important issues cannot continue.

HOW DO WE EDUCATE CITIZENS, AND WHAT DO THEY NEED TO KNOW?

If we can actually get the public's attention, what do they need to know and understand about the military and war? While research shows that the military is a highly respected, even revered, institution, the public knows next to nothing about how it is structured, how it operates, and the impact of never-ending wars on its people. Any institution—and the military is no exception—is made better by inspection, questioning, and even criticism. These represent an active interest, not just a slavish acceptance. Saying "Thank you for your service" is nice, but failing to question or even try to understand the military and its missions demonstrates a lack of interest and is ultimately a sign of disrespect. It does a disservice to those who choose to join the military. In this respect, America's education system has failed it.

There is a growing recognition that decades of neglect in the teaching of government and civics in our schools have created a national security problem. In previous decades, almost all students were required to take basic courses in the functioning of government as part of the school curriculum. Sadly, public education budgets have not kept pace, the requirements have been eliminated, and such courses have gradually disappeared. In an era when our institutions are under attack by disinformation campaigns, both from within the country and from without, the public is ill equipped to resist such attacks because it lacks even the most basic knowledge about those institutions. The National Commission on Military, National, and Public Service has recommended, among other things, that there be national standards for civics education and that institutions of higher learning take steps to improve such education at their institutions and the surrounding communities.[23]

At the university level, study of political science has done little to add to college students' general knowledge of government. The problem is that university scholars increasingly equate intellectual rigor with the use of models, simulations, and mathematical analysis and ignore questions of relevance more important to government decision makers.[24] Top-tier institutions attract top-tier talent in pertinent fields of national security. Unfortunately, much of the communication of scholars in these institutions is with other scholars, in arcane language understandable only by them. What is needed is a change in balance. Universities, while retaining their rigorous scholarship, must also attract experienced practitioners and talk and write about national security issues, not only for each other, but for the broader public as well. Universities educate students who will be the next generation of leaders. If they are to be of any real use to the nation, they must begin to focus on real-world issues and literacy in government affairs.

Citizens must take the time to educate themselves on issues affecting military forces and ask informed questions about the enormous sums of money spent on new weapons and force deployments. If they are uninterested, then Congress will be equally uninterested in reining in their profligacy or putting a check on the executive. Perhaps if the public had an understanding of the real costs of and reasons for war, there might be more resistance to US involvement in numerous conflicts, but someone first has to get their attention. Influential voices, including individuals and groups, must be able to overcome the inertia. They have to break through the cacophony of extraneous voices and set the tone of the conversation. They have to counter the argument that everything can be fixed by military force or the threat of its use.

Although America's wars are, in many ways, hidden from the public, we have to seek to understand the actual costs of war, in terms of both human costs and financial ones. Political leaders favoring conflict to solve problems never raise the issue of the human and financial costs of the wars they support or, if they do, tend to characterize them in glowing terms of quick, cheap, decisive, American victory. The reality is, of course, far different.

THE PERSONAL COST OF WAR

In recent years, the US has fought in countries where we had a clear and unchallenged advantage. While the conflicts were expensive, human losses were counted in the hundreds or thousands. In the future, conflicts could be against peer-competitor nations with all the advanced technologies similar to ours, or with emerging technological countries with advanced weapons, unlike what we faced during the long war on terror. The public needs to understand that the US can no longer assume a short and relatively bloodless war. The outcome of some easily imagined conflicts may actually be shocking—and shockingly expensive in treasure and lives—to the American people. The personal costs could be staggering.

The personal toll of war can only be described as heartbreaking. Long after the battles have been fought and the soldiers have returned home, the effects of war continue to be felt: families torn apart, bodies maimed, lives shattered, in many cases for causes that were unclear and only vaguely related to the security of the American people. Since the nation's founding, American war deaths alone number almost 1.2 million, with another 1.4 million wounded.[25] Focusing only on the post-9/11 wars in which the US has engaged, there have been seven thousand soldiers and sailors killed and another fifty-four thousand wounded. These are only the direct participants and do not count the innumerable innocent civilians killed or maimed as a result of the violence. Since 9/11, there have been approximately five hundred thousand killed in Afghanistan, Pakistan, and Iraq, including civilians, armed fighters, and local police.[26]

As world leaders threaten one another with military action and Western nuclear powers consider military action to prevent other countries from obtaining nuclear weapons, they must think very hard about the consequences of such actions. North Korea, while not equipped with the latest high-technology weapons, has an enormous standing army and thousands of artillery pieces and missiles aimed at South Korea—and the US forces stationed there. Their short- and medium-range missiles are capable and numerous. Now, with North Korea possessing a nuclear weapons capability, nuclear combat cannot be ruled out. A Korean War could be deadly—producing tens of thousands of deaths just in Seoul, and possibly a million casualties in the South alone. It would almost certainly be devastating physically in both the North and South.[27] US forces would take extremely heavy casualties defending South Korea. Would the American public consider such an outcome acceptable?

The US and its allies in the Middle East and Europe are rightfully concerned about the prospect of a nuclear-armed Iran, a country known to be a supporter of terrorism and fiercely anti-Israel. There is dangerously cavalier talk, however, about military action to prevent them from building nuclear weapons, weapons we have and weapons the world allowed North Korea to build, free from the threat of military intervention. No one, least of all an advocate for peace, wishes to see Iran or anyone else build nuclear weapons. However, leaders should be very cautious about precipitating a war with Iran. In recent months, the US and its allies have reportedly been responsible for the dangerously provocative assassinations of a high-ranking Iranian military officer and a top nuclear scientist. Al-Jazeera reporter Murtaza Hussain has cautioned,

> Public statements claiming that the extent of a conflict with Iran
> would be limited to targeted airstrikes on Iranian nuclear facili-

ties are utterly disingenuous, ignoring the escalating cycle of retribution that such limited conflicts necessarily breed. Crossing of the military threshold with Iran would also likely result in a far bigger conflagration than what politicians lead the public to believe. War with Iran would be no quick and clean affair, and would make the Iraq and Afghanistan wars, which cost trillions of dollars and the lives of thousands of soldiers and civilians, seem like a cakewalk.[28]

Escalation of the conflict, given the intense hatreds in the Middle East, would be almost assured. As we saw with Iraq, a war in the Middle East would likely last for years, with high numbers of casualties, combatants and noncombatants alike. The physical destruction would be enormous, and the economic consequences alone could be devastating for the average American.

Overseas contingency operations and ceaseless deployment cycles come at a great personal cost. They have caused problems of drug and alcohol abuse and have resulted in a depressingly high suicide rate among our troops. Individuals deployed to recent conflicts in Iraq and Afghanistan have shown significantly higher rates of substance abuse than civilians. They were far more likely to develop drug or alcohol abuse disorders than nondeployed service members who served during the same time period. Similar postdeployment increases in substance abuse problems have also been seen in Reserve and National Guard personnel.[29] Defense Department data show that the suicide rate in 2018 jumped sharply, with increases from 15 to 25 percent, depending on the service. Statistics for 2019 show an alarming 33 percent increase in air force suicides.[30] While statistics may tell us the magnitude of the problem, they do not begin to tell the true story of the postconflict hardships endured by soldiers and their families. It takes a visit to the military and veterans' hospitals to see the broken bodies and to really understand how lives are irrevocably altered by war.

THE FINANCIAL COST OF WAR

Military budgets, especially in the US, are simply enormous, and most citizens—even generally well-informed ones—have no idea of their size or how they are used. Historical data, when corrected for inflation, show that the US defense budget before 9/11 hovered around $500 billion, on average.[31] In the years since 9/11, those numbers have skyrocketed until now the defense budget sits at three-quarters of a trillion dollars annually. The decade following 9/11 saw defense budgets greater than any decade since the 1950s, a period that included far larger troop deployments.[32] Since 9/11, Congress has appropriated $1.6 trillion for overseas war operations alone.[33] Some estimates of the cost of the wars in Iraq and Afghanistan that include the Pentagon base budget, veterans' care and disability payments, increases in homeland security funding, foreign assistance, and interest payments peg the number at over $6 trillion.[34] War making and the military are expensive propositions. Yes, without question, our armed forces must be provided with the best equipment money can buy, but the excessive deployments and uses of those troops and that equipment create a heavy, and mostly unnecessary, financial burden on the taxpayer.

The size of the US military budget has significant effects on the economy. A large military budget contributes to budget deficits, inflation, and unfortunately, cuts to social welfare. Also, some economists conclude that increased spending on defense programs leads to decreases in private investment due to a bottleneck effect on capital.[35] Military spending displaces more productive government investment in high-tech industries, education, or infrastructure—all of which may affect long-term economic growth rates.[36] Even if the government did not spend another dollar on its wars, research shows that we will still have to pay a breathtaking $8 trillion extra in interest on past war borrowing by the 2050s. What if some of what we spend on weapons could instead be allocated to fixing our crumbling roads and bridges?

The defense budget represents approximately 16 percent of the federal budget, a substantial amount of money by any measure.[37] Citizens should be educated about what we are buying, why we are buying it, and how much it costs. What are the effects on taxes and productivity? What will go unfunded as a result? As President Eisenhower said about arms purchases in 1953, they are "in the final sense, a theft from those who hunger and are not fed, those who are cold and are not clothed."[38] His emotional appeal is now backed up by a significant amount of data. Research published in 2017 analyzed military spending by over 170 countries over the last forty-five years. The results showed that increased military spending consistently depresses a country's economic growth. The findings showed that over a twenty-year period, a 1 percent increase in military spending resulted in a decrease of 9 percent in economic growth.[39] Whether wars are paid for by taxation or debt, America's taxpayers have been burdened and the nation has experienced larger deficits, higher taxes, or inflation.[40] Unfortunately for our heirs, many of the serious financial effects present themselves to future generations as problems to solve. We are, as it were, mortgaging the future. Beyond a vague, but admittedly valuable, sense of security, military expenditures have no real residual value as capital investments. The protagonist of a late nineteenth-century war novel says, "The mechanism of the butt of a great gun which costs thousands of dollars in its making will soon be sold for only fourteen dollars and eighty cents, as old iron. . . . Even the genius of men . . . had been largely wasted."[41] Nineteenth-century writers recognized the waste of scientific talent engaged in war preparations. Imagine if even a fraction of the top scientists working on weapons technologies today could turn their attention to more pressing problems facing the world's populations. As Willard Fox wrote in 1966 at the height of the Vietnam War, "Economically, war is a waste. . . . It wastes manpower, capital goods, and raw materials . . . things that in the absence of war could be produced and consumed in ordinary peacetime life. . . . No amount of fiscal hocus pocus can change that reality."[42]

REASONS FOR WAR

Understanding the true costs of war is important, but as a prerequisite, citizens should care about and know the rationale behind going to war in the first place. Unfortunately, individual citizens spend too little time in critical thinking about such topics. They look largely to "elites" (in this case, perhaps their favorite media commentators) for information and opinions on the latest military adventures. MIT professor Adam Berinsky notes that "when political elites disagree as to the wisdom of intervention, the public divides as well. But when elites come to a common interpretation of political reality, the public gives them great latitude to wage war."[43] Such latitude should not be given so freely.

Individuals must be more questioning and better informed about foreign affairs and military issues. Politicians have become accustomed to using the military as a tool to implement their policies rather than as a force to defend our legitimate interests. The American public needs to inform itself about what its decision makers and military are doing. Unfortunately, the distance between the military and the people it serves has fueled the public's ignorance about how the military functions and is utilized. Our education system bears some responsibility for this. Among the most frightening and relevant findings of a 2016 survey was that almost 40 percent of respondents incorrectly said that the Constitution gives the president the power to declare war.[44] In a Hoover Institution–sponsored survey, a surprising number of respondents answered "don't know" to questions about the military's structure and use, lacking even the most rudimentary knowledge of the military, its culture, its basic structure, and its functions.[45] Without such understanding, they have no idea about the nature of the military and its relationship with civilian policy makers. It could be argued that when the public understands the costs of a military adventure balanced against its benefits they will opt for no intervention. The problem, however, is getting them to even think about such a trade-off in the first place. The answer may lie in a better and clearer explanation of the actual cost of our militarism, as opposed to the advertised, oft-repeated, political canards like *ensuring our freedom* and *protecting our way of life*.

The public should demand that political leaders explain the actual purpose and end goals of the military action—or the military investment in a new weapon such as the recently announced tactical nuclear weapon for the navy.[46] What is the mission and what are the priorities? Is the purpose to protect the homeland, protect our military and civilians overseas, protect our allies, protect access to resources, prevent genocide? Or are the goals more diffuse, such as projecting power or spreading democracy? Do the new weapons we seek to acquire have a war-fighting purpose or are they promoted just because the other side has them? These are important factors in the public decision to support military action. It should be made clear to the public why the decision makers wish to employ forces. Is there an immediate threat, an assumed threat, or a possible future threat? Is the war being considered one of necessity or one of choice? The fact that a country or group has the means to harm us is insufficient justification to resort to war.

There is substantial evidence that the decision calculus of politicians and policy makers is not always grounded in just questions of military and diplomatic efficiency and consequences. This raises important ethical concerns about national leaders' decisions to send troops into combat. A review of historical data shows that presidents were more likely to use force when their popularity was declining, to divert public attention from economic woes, or in the closing stages of the electoral process.[47] Detailed studies of a large number of crises have found that politics clearly influenced presidents' decisions to employ US military force.[48] The so-called diversionary theory suggests that leaders make use of the fact that constituencies become more cohesive during times of conflict. Scholars conclude that leaders divert attention away from domestic problems, such as a weak economy or sagging approval, by using force, thereby achieving what is known as "the rally effect."[49]

Leaders should have to explain why a particular military action is in the interests of the country. Why, for example, is it so important to prevent other countries from obtaining nuclear weapons that we will go to war to accomplish it? Or why is it actually essential that US naval forces not be intimidated by Chinese forces claiming sovereignty in the international waters of the South China Sea so essential for free global trade and shipping? The people should have some general idea of what the current rules of engagement are with these and other potential adversaries. The public should have some say about how aggressive, or not, we want our military posture to be.

As commentator Paul Pillar noted, often a form of "circular reasoning" plagues discussion of military deployments.[50] We get drawn into a conflict for some reason, then our forces are at risk, so we must deploy more forces to protect them—and on it goes. What is missing, he says, is a very basic process of actually defining and prioritizing US interests in a particular region and deciding how they might be harmed. Decisions to deploy forces go unchallenged. That the most fundamental questions about US involvement in foreign adventures—in which lives are lost—never even get asked is tantamount to criminal negligence.

At a very minimum, there should be a public discussion of the goals of military intervention and how it will end. What will success look like? Leaders should explain why such a deployment is actually in the interests of the US. What are we trying to achieve there? Why is it in our interests? What is the exit strategy? How will we know when the mission is complete and we can extricate ourselves? Former chairman of the Joint Chiefs of Staff General Colin Powell articulated a doctrine that called for the military to be deployed only when the objectives were clear, success was identifiable, and the military had a clear strategy to leave. Powell believed, on the basis of the Vietnam experience, that if the United States went to war, it should have a clear military objective: "I want to put the number of troops in that can take care of that problem, I want to have popular support, and I want to have an exit strategy. I want to go in, I want to accomplish it, and I want to get out."[51] We should not again make the mistake Secretary of Defense Donald Rumsfeld made in the 2003 invasion of Iraq when he said the military should go to war with the army it had. Future forces must be equipped with the technologies and weapons required to prevail in battle, or they should not be committed in the first place.

What must the public demand? For more than two decades, a majority of the public has consistently expressed the view that good diplomacy, rather than military strength, is the best way to ensure peace. Today, 61 percent say good diplomacy is the best way to ensure peace, while just 30 percent say military strength is the better approach.[52] If this is the case, why do we continually involve ourselves in military conflicts? More to the point, why do we allow our leaders to involve us in them? If the majority of the public is not in favor of conflict, why do we allow our leaders to engage in it? Why is there so little support for the State Department and the Foreign Service and so much largesse for the Department of Defense? The State Department has lost two-thirds of its career ambassadors and 20 percent of its experienced civil servants, while 15 percent of its positions abroad remain unfilled.[53] The administration's FY 2020 budget request calls for cuts in the international affairs budget, cuts in humanitarian assistance, and a $1 billion cut in funding for international organizations.[54]

The public should have a say as to whether we go to war with China over Taiwan or go to war with Russia over Ukraine, and it should have a say as to whether we go to war to prevent Iran from obtaining a nuclear weapon or to force North Korea to eliminate their nuclear and missile arsenal. Polls in the United States show that only a minority of Americans would favor US military personnel fighting to defend Taiwan.[55] Only 32 percent would support committing ground troops, and a mere 19 percent consider China as a military threat to Taiwan.[56] Even in Europe, which would be most affected by Russian aggression, only a minority of the population supports Article 5 of the NATO treaty calling on member states to come to the aid of another if it is attacked.[57] American polls showed that only 20 to 30 percent favored any kind of US military action to support Ukraine against Russian intervention.[58]

How can citizens stay informed as global engagements become increasingly complex, lightning-quick, and high-tech? The information openly available is rich and surprisingly plentiful. The public websites and public affairs offices of DARPA and IARPA (Intelligence Advanced Research Projects Activity) and the military service laboratories are informative and give an idea of what technologies are important to military planners. Organizations like the Federation of American Scientists and publications like the *Bulletin of the Atomic Scientists* provide dispassionate views of technology application to warfare without the self-promotion evident in many government publications.

Citizens should have a basic understanding of the military. There should be some understanding of its size, the different services, and their missions (to train and equip personnel for use in combat by regional combatant commanders). Understanding the missions of the regional and functional commands is critical. The US military has eleven combatant commands, each with a geographic or functional mission that provides command and control of military forces in peace and war. Functional commands operate worldwide and provide unique capabilities to geographic combatant commands and the military services, while geographic commands operate in clearly delineated areas and have a distinctive regional focus. What does Central Command do? What autonomy does the commander have in dealing with the warring factions in the Middle East? What is the role of Strategic Command? What authority does the commander have to release nuclear weapons? What about the reestablished Space Command, or the new

US Space Force? Who can order an attack on a space system? How do all of the commands interact with one another and with the secretary of defense and the president.? How are they equipped? How much of the defense budget goes to people, how much to operations, and how much to research and buying new weapons? Global affairs councils in major cities around the country and military affairs councils in cities and towns hosting military bases are excellent venues for citizens to learn more about issues or foreign and military affairs. Local National Guard and reserve units are great resources for more than just parades. They can provide education for schools and local civic organizations on military structure and missions. Universities are, of course, great repositories of knowledge and centers of expertise.

The Congressional Budget Office, the Government Accountability Office, and the Congressional Research Service are all nonpartisan and publish fact-based reports upon which members of Congress can rely to make decisions on military policy and funding. Think tanks, like the Brookings and Hoover institutions, while somewhat partisan leaning, can provide good debate about important military issues if consulted in parallel. Organizations like the Center for Strategic and International Studies and the Center for a New American Security provide in-depth analyses of foreign military issues, generally by former senior government officials. Finally, the National Academy of Sciences, the National Academy of Engineering, and the National Academy of Medicine conduct meticulously independent studies of major technology and policy issues affecting the military.

HOW DO WE GET THE ATTENTION OF THE PUBLIC?

What can be done to get the citizenry more engaged in foreign affairs and issues of the military? What can be done to get them to ask hard questions of political leaders and demand answers before American soldiers are engaged in armed conflict? Obviously, if the answers were simple, they would have been implemented by now. Indeed, the problem requires consideration of long-term as well as short-term action. The very first step in changing this situation must be to get the attention of the public. This is a multidimensional problem because what captures the interest of one segment of the population does not do so for another. Once we have their attention, we must educate citizens on the true costs of war and the dangers that new technologies present. While it is not precisely true that increased knowledge translates into better decisions by the public—other, less tangible, factors affect decision-making—accurate information is a necessary condition, even if itself insufficient.[59] If we are to ensure that the public is knowledgeable, the American education system will have to change.

FIXING FAILED CIVICS EDUCATION

The failure of the American education system, in general, is a topic of intense study and has been so for several decades. Much has been written about the lagging US performance in science, technology, engineering, and mathematics (STEM) and its negative impact on American productivity and standing in the world.[60] The failure of the system in the area of civics and knowledge of government has more recently been the subject of studies and reports.[61] Unlike the widespread concern over our STEM failures, however, our weakness in civics and government lacks the apparent real-time, near-term urgency so evident in failures in manufacturing or even weapons. Nonetheless, the continued lack of knowledge by citizens about their government, how it works, and how problems can and should be addressed will result in a slower, but inevitable, failure.

In 2012, the American Association of Colleges and Universities (AACU) published a report describing the "anemic civic health" in the US, noting, for example, that a test of civic literacy among college seniors resulted in an average, failing, score of just over 50 percent. The report described a widespread concern and recommended that civic learning and democratic engagement be raised to the level of national priorities. Americans need to understand how their political system works and how to influence it, but they also need to understand the cultural and global contexts in which our democracy operates. The AACU report was highly critical of American institutions of higher education, lamenting the fact that only a third of faculty promoted awareness of US or global social, political, or economic issues and only a third of students felt the need to become actively involved. The report called for colleges and universities to address campus culture, general education, and civic inquiry, as well as hands-on problem-solving.[62] University political science programs must, as discussed earlier, move beyond the trend toward quantitative studies and models employing advanced statistics, to more pressing, current problems and up-close student engagement.

CHANGING THE CONVERSATION

We have to start the process by changing the conversation from one of making war to one of maintaining peace. The strategy must, at its core, not let politicians completely control the narrative. For politicians wishing to use military forces, government public affairs offices aggressively distribute communications in support of military force and critical of those who oppose it. Propaganda is a powerful tool in the hands of the executive. Those who wish to resist the march to war must find a way to counter such messaging and to drive the conversation.

While we need to change the conversation, the people in charge must also change, the policies must change, and the technologies must change. The current generation of leaders got us into this mess. It is foolish to think they will get us out of it or even be inclined to try. The younger generation, on the other hand, has different values and motivations on which we must capitalize. We must change policies that allow politicians to involve us in wars with little explanation, and we must ensure that our systems are built to avoid conflict as a first priority. The technologies of war, as good as they are and as deeply intertwined with the decision-making process as they are, must be built to avoid war as the primary response.

While technology changes the environment and the elements of war, it remains important to look at the past causes and potential future causes of wars, and at the people who opposed them, and to speculate about how future war might be resisted. Are the old methods obsolete, or can they be adapted? How do we go about changing the conversation, controlling the narrative, making the discussion more about keeping the peace than preparing for war? Experience has shown time and again that only when public opinion becomes strong enough will world leaders even consider changing their behavior. When politicians fear for their political survival or dictators fear for the survival of their regime, the stage is at least set for the possibility of change.

THE ROLE OF INFLUENTIAL PEOPLE

The voices of some people matter more than those of others in shaping public opinion, and public opinion is critical in changing the behavior of politicians. Throughout history, statesmen and some military leaders, religious figures, and artists have made convincing cases for peace, sometimes giving their lives to such causes. These individuals have succeeded in changing public sentiment and pressuring leaders to forgo violence or bring an end to conflicts. Now, in a highly connected and interdependent world, the question remains: Is it possible to do so again?

Today, public intellectuals, who in the past were powerful in shaping public opinion about important topics, are rare or nonexistent. There is an extensive body of literature on the topic, but simply put, the dearth is caused in part by the increased specialization over time of academia, in part by the sheer volume and number of voices—some well informed and some merely useless—enabled largely by the internet, and in part by a long-existing strain of anti-intellectualism and mistrust of expertise by populist politicians and the public. There remain, however, influential individuals in business, the arts, entertainment, and even sports. They can be called upon and could make a major difference in political behavior. The public has a fascination with popular figures: movie stars, sports figures, internet "influencers," heroic figures like astronauts, explorers, larger-than-life business figures like Elon Musk, and so on. Curiously, even nonscientists are fascinated by the Nobel Prizes and follow closely the announcements of the winners each year. One by-product of this hero worship is that these individuals gain overnight credibility, whether deserved or not, with millions of observers who hang on their every word.[63] Celebrities take on the status of sages. Celebrity and a public platform from which to influence citizens have long been understood as necessary to affect change. In the late nineteenth and early twentieth centuries—a time when antiwar sentiment was already high—such figures as Bertha von Suttner in Germany and Jane Addams in the US commanded large followings and wrote extensively about the dangers of militarism. Today, Greta Thunberg, a teenage environmental activist, commands enormous attention and influences the behavior of governments.

Bertha von Suttner, born in Prague in 1843, wrote prolifically about peace and disarmament, becoming a highly prominent figure in the pacifist movement after publishing her most famous work, the novel *Lay Down Your Arms,* a work of fiction that described the brutal realities and impacts of war. [64] Like many before her, and after, she argued that the continued buildup of armaments only encouraged their use. She worked tirelessly against national and religious fanaticism, social injustice, human rights violations, and discrimination against women. She was the subject of intense criticism and ridicule among industrialists and male chauvinists. She was awarded the Nobel Peace Prize in 1905.

Jane Addams was a major figure in American and international peace movements, becoming an antiwar activist in 1899 following the Spanish-American War. Her influential 1907 book *Newer Ideals of Peace* combined the concepts of social justice with ideas from pacifist thinking.[65] Addams founded the Women's International League for Peace and Freedom in 1919 and worked for many years to get the great powers to disarm and conclude peace agreements. She was a tireless supporter and defender of human rights, speaking and writing passionately about the pervasive militarism in society and urging governments to use their energies and resources for the common good and welfare rather than war. During World War I, she chaired a women's conference for peace held in the Hague in the Netherlands. When the US entered the war, Addams spoke out loudly against it, actions for which she was deemed a dangerous radical and a danger to security. She, too, faced harsh criticism from the public and the media for her pacifism. She was awarded the Nobel Peace Prize in 1931.

The philosopher Bertrand Russell was an outspoken critic of preparations for war and campaigned vigorously against British participation in World War I. He was ultimately jailed and lost his position at Trinity College as a result of his activism. Opposed to war from early on, he spent his career writing and speaking out against war hysteria and rabid nationalism and in the 1950s and 1960s engaged in political causes primarily related to nuclear disarmament and opposition to the Vietnam War. He coauthored the 1955 Manifesto with Albert Einstein, calling for nuclear disarmament. Russell was awarded the Nobel Prize for Literature in 1950 for his writings in support of "humanitarian ideals and freedom of thought."

Linus Pauling is known popularly for his controversial 1970s claims about the curative properties of Vitamin C. He was, however, a serious and accomplished scientist, awarded the Nobel Prize for Chemistry in 1954. Pauling was also a peace activist, strongly opposed to nuclear weapons, and a signatory to the Russell-Einstein Manifesto in 1955. He continued to speak out against war, taking controversial stands against the Vietnam conflict as well. For his antiwar stance, Pauling was labeled a communist and was criticized by the government and some of his peers, several times having his passport revoked. He was awarded the Nobel Peace Prize in 1962.

Andrei Sakharov was a Russian theoretical physicist widely known and lauded as the father of the Soviet hydrogen bomb. Beginning in the 1950s, however, he became critical of Soviet abuses of human rights and began to speak and write against the consequences of the nuclear arms race. Sakharov was essentially placed under house arrest for his activities until 1985. He was awarded the Nobel Peace Prize in 1975.

Lech Walesa was a labor union leader in Gdansk, Poland, when that country was a member of the Warsaw Pact with the Soviet Union. Walesa was successful in negotiating for better conditions when his Solidarity union went on strike in 1980. For his union-organizing efforts, he was frequently placed under surveillance and was several times arrested by communist authorities. Ultimately, when the USSR and the Warsaw Pact dissolved, he was elected president of Poland. For his efforts in support of workers' rights and against communist oppression, Walesa was awarded the Nobel Peace Prize for 1983.

In 1963, Vaclav Havel, a playwright in the former Czechoslovakia, published his first play, a satire about the dehumanizing nature of communist dogma. He continued to write plays advocating for human rights. Under Soviet influence, his plays were banned, and he was arrested and served a prison sentence for his criticism of the regime. After the collapse of the Czechoslovakian communist government in 1989, Havel was elected president of Czechoslovakia. Havel did not receive a Nobel Prize for his important contributions. However, he is widely remembered for his pivotal role in toppling communism in his homeland.

It is worth noting that many of the individuals who have spoken out for peace and against war have been treated as disloyal. Somehow, in a severely warped logic, being against war has often been deemed unpatriotic, as if militarism and patriotism were synonymous. Supporters of US war policies have repeatedly conflated dissent with disloyalty, often restricting freedom of speech and suppressing open expressions of opposition.[66] Appeals to patriotism have allowed politicians to whip up war frenzy and depict their opponents as disloyal, many times resorting to abusive measures to silence opposition. In a period that Thomas Jefferson referred to as the "reign of witches," John Adams and the Federalists in 1798 used the Alien and Sedition Acts to squelch opposition to a war with France.[67] In the Civil War, Abraham Lincoln suspended habeas corpus, and in World War I, Woodrow Wilson implemented the Sedition Act, imprisoning several thousand opponents of the war.[68] In the aftermath of World War II and the advent of McCarthyism and rabid anticommunism, the scientists who had developed the atomic bomb and had begun to speak of limiting nuclear weapons suddenly came under suspicion and oppression as possible enemies of the state. Top theoretical physicists were targeted by the House Un-American Activities Committee (HUAC) and were accused of being threats to national security.[69] The *Bulletin of the Atomic Scientists*, initiated to inform the public about the dangers of the nuclear arms race, was considered subversive and subjected to government censorship.[70] Early Vietnam antiwar protesters at Kent State University, site of a later deadly shooting of students by National Guard troops, were attacked by prowar students, newspapers spoke out against them, police and federal agents surveilled them, and town residents thought they were communists, unpatriotic, and un-American.[71] Then vice president Spiro Agnew called antiwar activists "anarchists and communists who detest everything about this country and want to destroy it,"[72] going so far as to accuse them of sedition.[73] Senator Eugene McCarthy, an unsuccessful candidate for the Democratic nomination for president in 1968, was labeled as unpatriotic and un-American for his stand against the Vietnam War.[74] What is consistent among the peace activists is the doggedness and determination to continue and their unwillingness to allow obstacles to deter their pursuit of peace. What are we to make of the current sad state of affairs in which those speaking out against war are vilified as the enemy, while all military personnel are considered heroes—whether they have served in combat or not?

Since the end of the Cold War, concerns by many activists about excessive militarism have grown and are now combined with worries about social justice, including racism, immigration, and environmentalism. And once again, those environmental and other activists are attacked and criticized.[75] Their motives and even their characters are called into question. In shameful displays of verbal abuse against young people, some political pundits questioned the motives and sincerity of survivors of the Parkland High School shooting who were demonstrating for gun control legislation,[76] and the young climate activist Greta Thunberg is labeled by nonsupportive media outlets as "evil" and "mentally ill."[77]

It is worth noting that antiwar sentiment has always been particularly strong among women and that women have repeatedly played a critical role in raising public awareness and concern about militarism and the country's involvement in war. Women have often succeeded where men have failed to take control of the conversation and shape the public narrative about the horrors of war. The importance of women in peace activism, as evidenced by their numerous Nobel Peace Prizes among other honors, is enormous. Of the total of Nobel Peace Prizes, women received the award only three times during its first seventy years, but fourteen times in the last forty-five years. While the numbers are not large, the trend reflects the growing influence of women on socially important issues. Women have a unique perspective, as the burden of war falls heavily upon them. Their roles as mothers and spouses are critical to this perspective. In the US, groups such as Code Pink and the Raging Grannies are visible examples. In Europe during the Cold War, the Women of Greenham Common played a major role in keeping press interest on stopping the deployment of medium-range nuclear missiles. The performances of these groups imply that women's traditional roles as mothers and caregivers give women the moral authority and moral obligation to fight against violence and war, drawing attention to the differential impact of war on women.[78] It is noteworthy that when women are in decision-making roles with regard to war, it is less likely that war will result. One study found that when the percentage of women lawmakers increased by 5 percent, the state was five times less likely to resort to violence.[79]

It has not been just writers, activists, and academics speaking out against continued wars. Many who have actually experienced the horror of war speak out against it. General George C. Marshall, having served with distinction in World War II as chief of staff of the US Army and after the war as secretary of state, was also a highly credible and eloquent advocate for peace. He was the architect of the well-known Marshall Plan, which helped rebuild the destroyed enemy countries. He was awarded the Nobel Peace Prize in 1954. Adding credibility to the antiwar message, World War I veterans spoke out against war, including Erich Maria Remarque, author of *All Quiet on the Western Front*, in Germany and, in the US, Ernest Hemingway, author of *A Farewell to Arms*. The US in World War II, notwithstanding the common view of that conflict as the "good war," had Kurt Vonnegut's *Slaughterhouse Five* and Joseph Heller's *Catch-22* to describe—from personal experience—the absurdity and brutality of that war. Army veteran Tim O'Brien and marine veteran Karl Marlantes speak forcefully of the insanity of the Vietnam War in *The Things They Carried* and *What It's Like to Go to War,* respectively. But where are these heroic voices today? Where are the George C. Marshalls? US Army major Danny Sjursen attributes the deafening silence to the all-volunteer nature of the US military. In his view, soldiers today think that to criticize is to seem unpatriotic. The good officer is stoic and soldiers on. Sjursen, who lost seven men to combat and to suicide in the wars in Iraq and Afghanistan, says that "their banal sacrifice demands explanation. They deserve as much."[80]

Religious groups and individuals have long played a major role in advocating against war. Aquinas and Augustine were leading figures in just war theory, the Quakers have long been opposed to war, and Catholic popes—at least in the modern era—have actively sought to prevent or end violent conflicts. The Second Vatican Council (1962–65) called upon Catholics to undertake a "completely fresh reappraisal of war." In 1983, the US Conference of Catholic Bishops spoke out forcefully against nuclear weapons and nuclear war.[81] Pope Francis, in his 2017 World Day of Peace message, makes an unmistakable point, saying that "we should no longer damn nonviolence with faint praise by recognizing it only as a heroic witness for saints, or as a tactic we recommend to protesters only when we fear their desperation will turn violent and upset our comfortable lives." Instead, as Francis implies, nonviolence must become normal and natural to us—must become our very "style of politics."[82]

MOVEMENTS

In each period of conflict, there are individuals, organized and ad hoc groups, statesmen, and writers who speak out and actively oppose war. Critically, in almost all cases, these individuals and groups have garnered public attention and succeeded in creating an alternative narrative to the war fervor (or apathy) that got us into conflict in the first place. The important thing to note is that this is a long-term effect.

While individual voices are often effective, sometimes there are none who alone can capture the attention of the public. It is at those times that like-minded individuals coalesce into groups with a common goal. Again, Reinhold Niebuhr: "There is always in every nation, a body of citizens more intelligent than the average, who see the issues between their own and other nations more clearly than the . . . patriot. . . . Although it may at times place a check upon the more extreme types of national self-seeking, it is usually not powerful enough to affect national attitudes in a crisis."[83]

Peace activists march, protesters rally, movements form—and wars continue to be fought. They did not stop World War I. They did not stop the Vietnam War. They did not prevent the invasion of Iraq. Why, then, if peace and antiwar movements fail to prevent or end wars, should they persist? Are protests and antiwar activism wasted efforts? Absolutely not. Peace movements and antiwar campaigns are never solely about immediate results. What is important is that they can—and do—influence public opinion. It is important to take a longer-term view. While it is unrealistic to think that peace activism and peace movements will have an immediate impact, it is entirely plausible that they will fundamentally change the conversation and the public's attitudes. These activities often do not result in immediate change, but the differences they make are complex, are often subtle, and take time to manifest themselves. While they often fail to attain immediate goals, they do create lasting change in political debates, political institutions, and the wider culture.[84] They become part of a longer-term effort at laying the foundations for citizens to better understand the need for peace and cooperation rather than war and confrontation. An element of such lasting change includes, for instance, limitations on decision makers who would resort to violence. The outcry against chemical warfare in World War I resulted in the Chemical and Biological Toxin Convention. The campaign for nuclear disarmament in the 1960s resulted in a series of strategic arms treaties. Antiwar sentiment, while very widespread, did not have a large impact on the Vietnam conflict until later in the war, when protests led to public disillusionment and ultimate US withdrawal. The peace movement was unsuccessful in preventing the 2003 invasion of Iraq, but its arguments and predictions of a long and protracted conflict were shown to be correct. The movement was vocal and widespread and contributed to the turning of the public against the policies of the Bush administration. It elevated the role of civil society as an increasingly important voice in matters of war and peace.[85] Peace movements can act as important governors on the use of executive powers.[86]

During the Civil War, there was resistance on both sides. The North experienced very high draft evasion rates. The South experienced desertion, active resistance, and insurrection. In the North, there were conscientious objectors, pacifists, and antidraft rioters. In the South, there were anti-Confederate and antiwar organizations, draft evaders and deserters who undermined the Confederacy through guerrilla warfare, spies for the Union, and attacks on conscription offices.[87] Obviously the war ground to a grim conclusion, but these activities served to impede, if only for a while, the war efforts of both sides. Perhaps even a few lives were spared. In the Spanish-American War, while the public was swayed by the so-called yellow journalism of the time, realists tried in vain to stop the war. One industry leader summarized the position of the industrialists by saying, "The antiwar class comprises... the industrialist, the merchant, the railroad investor. . . . The interests on whom the country is dependent for its daily bread . . . are almost unanimously against war."[88]

At present, there are few effective movements against the ongoing wars around the world. Antiwar movements today are essentially moribund. No large-scale war is being fought, but the killing continues in multiple, smaller-scale, often secret, wars out of the public eye. Wars of today have little impact on the individual citizen and create no sense of outrage. Younger generations of Americans seem to have concluded that antiwar activism isn't worth the effort. For them, war has been a part of their entire lives. They are not personally at risk, and they have too many other problems at home, like college costs, health care, and climate change. Fortunately, there are other ways to get the public to think about war.

THE IMPACT OF LITERATURE, POETRY, MUSIC, AND ART

Closely tied to the antiwar activists and movements are the forms of popular culture and entertainment extant during the period of a conflict. Literature has always played a key role, as have poetry and music. In the modern era, radio, television, and the internet have provided ever-faster modes of distribution for these things. Social media platforms are enormously influential and effective.

The role literature plays in society is the subject of much scholarly debate. Some believe it reflects society, while others think it influences or shapes society. In the first case, the idea is that literature reveals the essential world outlook of a culture, representing its basic norms and values. It may confirm and strengthen ideas, but it acts primarily as an index of cultural change, a symptom, not a cause. The alternative view naturally sees literature as shaping society and sees artists as agents of social change. In this view, literature produces the conception of ideas that precede and guide political movements.[89] Likely, the answer lies somewhere in between. Literature plays a powerful role in both reflecting and shaping public opinion. Regardless of the genre, whether serious exposé, history, biography, or fiction, that which finds intense interest among readers will likely determine the prevailing mood in a society. As one author said, literature enables us to see the world through the eyes of others and could, in fact, help us to modify a too-narrow worldview.[90] Literature, art, poetry, music— and their current forms so amplified by new technology—are a means to quickly influence the public, if properly employed, by conveying the awful realities of war.

Antiwar sentiment in literature is far from a new phenomenon. While many historical writings seem to glorify individual exploits and heroism, there are numerous comments about the suffering caused by war, and a strong desire for peace evident throughout ancient Greek literature, for example. *The Iliad* is in one sense a war story and in another sense a scathing indictment of the effects of war.[91] Anti–Trojan War literature characterized war as frivolous, unnecessary, and stupid. Homer writes that war is a result of greed and hate and creates confusion, destruction, and death, while peace permits happiness, prosperity, and justice.[92]

In the period preceding World War I—a period that saw the rapid industrialization and dehumanization of war—antiwar literature received wide public acceptance. Many authors openly questioned the morality of warfare and worked to change the images of war and battles as fields of honor and glory. In the aftermath of World War I, Vera Brittain wrote in 1930, "How to preserve the memory of our suffering in such a way that our successors may understand it and refrain from the temptations offered by glamour and glory—that is the problem which we, the war generation, have still to solve before the darkness covers us."[93] American antiwar writers in World War I forced readers to confront the grim realities of warfare. Their goal was to remove the romanticism and hero worship that pervaded so much contemporary writing about war. They wanted to instead highlight war's nature and to present an unsparing and disturbing image of it. War, they insisted, was simply a test of endurance, not valor.[94]

Tim O'Brien, a Vietnam veteran, writes that war has no clarity and that "the only certainty is absolute ambiguity."[95] Philip Caputo's *A Rumor of War,* a personal tale of his time in Vietnam, was what William Styron called a "searching meditation on the ambivalent discord that warfare can create in the hearts of decent men."[96] Iraq War veteran and English professor Roy Scranton, author of the novel *War Porn,* depicts the absurdity of war, as well as the needless brutality, and writes scathingly about the political and bureaucratic maneuverings that get us into war in the first place.[97] He speaks bluntly about the myths we tell ourselves and the justifications we create about our motives for so often resorting to war. Scranton, one reviewer said, conveys the "surreal feel of modern war—where real-life bleeds into nightmare."[98]

Present-day authors do not address issues of war and peace in the way that authors in past periods of conflict did. Unlike the horrendously destructive wars experienced by those authors, the wars of today's developed nations have become smaller scale, with less manpower and more advanced technology. The many operations that followed the Iraq War and became the global war on terror were smaller and less visible. Terrible as they are for the victims of those wars, these operations do not capture the imagination in the same way larger conflicts do. In any event, the reading public is insulated from even these wars by the presence of the all-volunteer military.[99] There are no draftees, and writer-veterans find no large understanding reading public who share the insanity of their experiences. The reader experiences war only vicariously. Today's soldier is a highly trained and disciplined professional who volunteered for combat duty. Why, the thinking must go, would he or she write anything about it, particularly anything critical?

Music has long played a key role in the expression of antiwar sentiment. During the Civil War, songs calling for peace or expressing general dismay at the horror of war appeared while the war was going on. Some of these are thought to be the beginnings of what we know today as peace songs used to protest warfare. The song "Let Us Have Peace" by Will S. Hayes in 1861 approached the issue by asserting that brothers should not fight brothers, and it generally called for reconciliation.[100] Some songs pled for peace indirectly by telling stories that shed light on the senselessness of war.[101] After World War I, the music of Edward Elgar and Vaughn Williams evoked the sadness and terrible horror of that conflict.[102] Elgar's 1919 *Cello Concerto* was a brooding and melancholy reflection on the war, and Williams's 1931 *Symphony No. 4* was a fierce antiwar statement. Lest antiwar movements develop and thrive in those authoritarian situations, in Mao Zedong's China, any music that did not serve the goals of the state was banned. In the Soviet Union, all music intended for publication had to be approved by official censors.[103] In the US during the Vietnam War, songs played a key role in sustaining the sentiment of the antiwar movement. Pete Seeger's "Where Have All the Flowers Gone" captured the prevailing mood of the growing number of protesters and members of the public, describing the increasing casualties of war and repeating the refrain "When will they ever learn?"[104]

Art has also served as a strong indictment of war. Rubens's 1638 work *Consequences of War* depicted the horrors of the Thirty Years' War. Christopher Nevinson's 1917 painting *Paths to Glory* is a depressing rendition of death on the battlefields of World War I. Picasso's 1937 masterpiece *Guernica* was a powerful reminder of the suffering wrought by the Spanish Civil War. As Charles Andrews reminds us, "The creative visions of pacifist revolutionaries who imagined nonviolent alternatives to war . . . may be worthy of inspiration."[105]

TARGETING THE MOTIVATIONS OF THE NEXT GENERATION OF LEADERS

An appeal to a newer set of values, different from those of the generation that got us into this mess, would seem to be a good place to interest the new generation of leaders. The motivations of the younger generations are different from those of people currently in positions of authority who are aging baby boomers and Cold War veterans. The millennials and Gen X cohorts put far less value on hierarchical structures and have far less interest in politics and interstate rivalries. They are interested in the related topics of human rights and racism, rational immigration policies, health, poverty and economic inequality, education, and the environment and climate change. Social inequality is among the major issues for the millennial generation.[106] The millennial generation is more tolerant, open to change, and more global in outlook.[107] Of critical importance is the fact that they are less supportive than their elders of assertive national security policy.[108] When asked about the seriousness of such issues as conflict or even large-scale war, only about a third of people aged eighteen to thirty-five identified them as among the most serious. Why, they asked, should we spend so much effort and treasure on foreign adventures when we have so many problems to solve here at home?[109] Of that same age group of young people, 45 percent said climate change and natural resources were the most serious global issues.[110] Seventy percent of those under fifty-five years of age were concerned about global warming compared to 56 percent among those fifty-five and older.[111] Like nuclear weapons in a previous era, climate change is viewed as an existential threat, albeit a longer-term one. It will be important to make the connection between these topics and their importance to questions of peace and war if the young generations are ever to be motivated to actively resist war.

POLICY, LEGAL, AND INSTITUTIONAL CHANGES

ARMS CONTROL

Technological development will continue to outpace social, legal, and institutional changes to accommodate it.[112] This is unfortunately also true in the arena of arms control. Governments and international institutions are finding it difficult to manage the introduction of new or in-development war-fighting technologies.[113] While there is growing public discussion by senior government officials about ethical issues of new weapon systems and AI, there is little tangible progress in policy development or arms control and nonproliferation efforts. One group of experts in artificial intelligence and autonomous systems has concluded that the lack of policy consensus in those areas poses real risks. They explain that without such agreed-to norms, states could fall victim to untested or unsafe weapons, widespread proliferation, and illicit use by malevolent actors.[114] Many Americans find it hard to believe that cyber incidents or proxy wars could end up in a nuclear confrontation. However, distorted and artificially amplified perceptions of the threats, complex and poorly understood weapons and technologies, and a lack of rules and norms of behavior may lead to unwanted and unexpected violence.[115] While we have treaties for nuclear, chemical, and biological weapons, no such agreements exist for space or cyber, or have even been considered as a means to control the weaponization of artificial intelligence and autonomy. The issue is urgent. Nations are racing to achieve superiority and will inevitably implement the technologies with the absolute minimum amount of testing and experience.

One of the ways we can avoid conflict is through the development of international agreements, short of formal treaties, and through meaningful arms control and counterproliferation discussions. Just the opposite is happening. George W. Bush previously withdrew the US from the Anti-Ballistic Missile (ABM) treaty. In recent years, the US has withdrawn from the Joint Comprehensive Plan of Action (JCPOA) with Iran, the Intermediate Nuclear Forces (INF) Treaty, and the Open Skies Treaty. Fortunately, the new US administration has chosen to extend the New START Treaty to allow time for renewed arms control talks. Further threatening strategic stability, the US, China, and Russia are all in intense competition in the new war-fighting domains and technologies, making it all the more important to at least establish domain-specific norms to prevent a miscalculation or misunderstanding. During the entire Cold War, the US and the USSR raced to build staggering numbers of enormously destructive weapons but were at the same time engaging in a series of successful arms control treaties.

There are those today who argue that the old order is incapable of accommodating the power shifts that are being introduced by the new technologies. The argument is that the old structures to limit proliferation of nuclear weapons will not work with new technologies because they are so widely diffused into multiple systems. Additionally, the argument goes, global norms of ethics and behavior may be harder to establish as new, less powerful, players seek to gain technological advantage.[116] The more ready availability of these technologies means that the established global players can no longer enforce agreed-to norms. All of this is true enough, but that does not mean that we should give up trying. The mere act of trying to identify key, problematic technologies for control is valuable. And when the major world powers commit to nonproliferation goals, lesser powers often will follow. For example, if the US and other major powers commit to working on developing norms and principles to guide and possibly constrain research, development, and eventual deployment of autonomous weapons systems, those norms could help establish expectations about legally or ethically appropriate conduct.[117] In talking about the dangers of artificial intelligence, author Paul Scharre writes that the US should begin discussions with both China and Russia to identify AI applications that pose unacceptable risks of escalation or loss of control and work to reduce those risks. "The biggest danger for the United States in an AI race," he says, "is not losing but creating a world in which no one wins."[118]

For now, the Tallinn Manual comes as close as anything to establishing norms of cyber behavior. A product of a three-year project by twenty renowned international law scholars and practitioners, the

Tallinn Manual identifies the international law applicable to cyber warfare and proposes rules to govern such conflicts. It addresses topics including sovereignty, state responsibility, jus ad bellum, international humanitarian law, and the law of neutrality. An attempt by the United Nations group of government experts to agree to a treaty on cyber behavior failed in 2017. The US, China, and Russia all express a desire to negotiate but stay stubbornly wedded to their old demands and mistrust of the other parties. The sad lack of strategic imagination presents a danger to the world.

We have the venerable Outer Space Treaty, agreed on in 1967, but it is far too general and too old to address newer threats in space like co-orbital inspector satellites and rendezvous and proximity operations, or threats caused by debris. We need rules of the road for space like those we have for maritime operations. Space norms, such as limiting debris, avoiding collisions, and sharing space surveillance information, can reduce the likelihood of accidents and protect valuable orbital regimes. All who operate in space would benefit from a more safe, predictable, and efficient operating environment. Joan Johnson-Freese, a professor at the US Naval War College, has said that "if space diplomacy got a quarter of the attention that space warfighting does, I think we would be a lot better off. But that doesn't go along with great power competition and kind of chest-thumping announcements."[119] Norms can serve to highlight abnormal behavior, enabling warning of and protection against threats. While norms will not prevent a committed aggressor from deliberately disrupting or denying space services, they may be enough to dissuade a rational actor from routinely engaging in irresponsible acts. Norms, then, can form the basis of criteria for early indications and warning of potentially aggressive actions. Military space forces might not like the idea of rules that will constrain their freedom of action in space, but in other domains militaries already accept legally binding constraints, having embraced international humanitarian law (also known as the law of war or the law of armed conflict) and have translated those laws into rules of engagement that guide service members. Space should be no different.

How do we avoid a space war, a cyber war, a proxy war, or war with a nuclear Iran? How do we avoid war against China if they invade Taiwan? If Chinese hackers disrupt our power grid? If Russia invades

Estonia or some other NATO country? One simple answer to these questions is that we must keep talking to our adversaries. Even in the darkest days of the Cold War, Russia and the US maintained military-to-military connections as well as strong diplomatic communications. Such communications are greatly diminished today. Following Russia's actions in Crimea and Ukraine, the US inexplicably did just the opposite, cutting off all government-to-government discussions on arms control. Tensions have grown worse, yet there is little meaningful dialogue, and there are diminishing means by which to have one. Communications channels set up during the Cold War to help keep crises from spinning out of control have been eliminated or badly maintained.[120]

At the height of the Cold War, psychologist Charles Osgood formulated a new approach to international relations called "Graduated Reciprocation in Tension Reduction," or GRIT.[121] Osgood's psychology-based approach consisted of a series of carefully calibrated, reciprocal, confidence-building steps that would gradually foster greater trust between the two superpowers. Mikhail Gorbachev and George H. W. Bush successfully employed such an approach, which ultimately ended (temporarily at least) the insane nuclear arms race. We seem to have completely lost interest in fostering trust. Quite the contrary, many of our actions and those of other countries are intended to destroy trust. It is essential that, if we cannot stop the major powers from developing some of the dangerous new weapon technologies, we must attempt to prevent their proliferation into the hands of dangerous nations and groups. There needs to be a multilateral or bilateral discussion of treaties, conventions, nonproliferation agreements, and verification regimes for these weapons. The State Department is essential, and there is enormous value in ongoing negotiations with competitors and adversaries at the diplomatic and military levels. Such discussions should also include escalation prevention, especially now in this era of highly automated command and control. This is an argument for so-called *technical confidence-building measures*. Russia expert Peter Zwack says that what will be required is "direct, quiet, and patient dialog coupled with unambiguous actions that will promote mutual understanding."[122] What are needed to ensure effective crisis management are clear signals of self-restraint.

Lack of trust, or trust betrayed, can end in tragedy. In 1837, Honoré de Balzac, as a part of his *Human Comedy,* wrote a story entitled "A Passion in the Desert."[123] In it, a panther and a soldier find themselves stranded and facing one another in the desert of Algeria. The soldier could kill the panther, or the panther could eat the soldier, but neither happens. They warily eye each other and move carefully about in their confined circumstance. They are together in a state of unstable equilibrium, in which they have the option of lowering the tension or turning violently on one another. As the story progresses, the two develop something of a relationship through a series of confidence-building actions. As the soldier ruminates on the story in his old age, he questions the events that led to the sad, tragic ending in which, as a result of a wholly ambiguous move by the panther, he killed the cat to whom he had become a cautious friend. We must find ways to maintain the equilibrium and avoid killing one another.

As General Marshall said about relations between armed nations, "Perhaps the most important single factor will be a spiritual regeneration to develop goodwill, faith, and understanding among nations. Economic factors will undoubtedly play an important part. Agreements to secure a balance of power, however disagreeable they may seem, must likewise be considered. And with all these, there must be wisdom and the will to act on that wisdom."[124] Marshall understood that disproportionate power on one side causes resentment and fear in the less powerful. Imbalances in power and capabilities create dangerous instabilities. The reaction of the Soviet Union and now Russia to US investment in missile defense systems is a classic example. While a nation or other entity may not have malevolent intentions toward another, when faced with the prospect that its adversary may have sufficient power to overwhelm it, it will seek to redress the imbalance, thus perpetuating the cycle of dangerous arms races.

AUTHORIZATION TO USE MILITARY FORCE AND WAR POWERS

Much has been written about the so-called imperial presidency and the balance of war powers between Congress and the executive. Many have lamented the almost-total powerlessness and unwillingness of

Congress to challenge the president's war-making ability. If we are to have any hope of slowing or putting a check on the use of force, however, voters must demand that their congressional representatives actively engage in issues of war, and Congress must regain and reassert its power to restrain the executive in the conduct of war, via the authorization to use military force (AUMF). It must stop hiding behind the president and stand for an explicit decision. Sadly, the American public is ambivalent when it comes to war. Americans claim in opinion polls to prefer no military involvement in foreign adventures, yet they easily acquiesce to its permanence in our foreign policy. This ambivalence exists because the public is largely shielded from military issues. Members of Congress do not want to go on record as authorizing a war, so they allow the president to conduct military operations unchecked. Politicians from both parties reacted angrily to a recent administration decision to assassinate an Iranian general, but after a flurry of activity did nothing to limit the president's power. The money to pay for our wars is borrowed from future generations, yet Congress continues to appropriate huge sums both for new systems and for overseas operations. The average American does not have to worry about engaging personally in our multiple wars, and we are quite satisfied to let a small percentage of our country bear the burden of service.[125]

PAYING FOR OUR WARS

The public feels that in general the overall level of defense spending is adequate or slightly too high. Polls indicate tepid support for military engagement around the globe. However, while Americans may have general views on the subject, they know little about the major elements of the defense budget or how funding for overseas military operations is allocated.[126] They should, and they need to have a say in those decisions. As described earlier, in one way or another, the public ends up paying for our foreign adventures. It makes sense that the most meaningful issues facing citizens are so-called pocketbook issues, those affecting family budgets and livelihoods. War is a pocketbook issue, but the public fails to realize it. If politicians wish to use military force, it should require that such use be paid for explicitly and that each citizen be given an accurate accounting of the costs and sources of funding. As it is, the average American family is unaffected by our wars. The government demands nothing from the public, and that is what it gets—nothing. No new taxes are levied to pay for them. Perhaps if they were, they might generate actual concern and interest in those wars.[127]

Before the Vietnam War, US wars were paid for by either war bonds or taxes. We must return to fiscal responsibility where war is concerned. Sarah E. Kreps, of Cornell University, says of the financing of America's frequent, seemingly never-ending conflicts that "contemporary wars are all put on the nation's credit card, and that eliminates a critical accountability link between the populace and the conduct of war." Wars, she says, no longer have a political cost to elected leaders because they do not come with an obvious financial cost to taxpayers. Therefore, wars can rage for years on end because they do not have a meaningful impact on the average person's life and there is no sense of shared sacrifice.[128] The requirement for up-front funding of overseas deployments could easily be added to the authorization process embodied in the AUMF.

CONSCRIPTION

During ancient Rome's heyday, its citizens felt a personal stake in the success of the empire. Citizens had rights but also accepted that they had duties and responsibilities. During times of crisis, Rome could call on all of its citizens to come to the rescue.[129] A core of the problem today is that while citizens expect much of their government, they are unwilling to provide much in return. They appear unwilling to satisfy their part of the "social contract" about which Jean-Jacques Rousseau wrote in 1762. While much of what he wrote concerned the responsibilities of the state to its citizens, he also spoke of the "general will" and the contributions of each citizen to it. Rousseau strongly supported the idea of the state and encouraged patriotism among its citizens.[130]

The simplest solution, if we are going to continue to fight endless wars, might be that the US have some form of conscripted service. More to the point, perhaps, if we had mandatory military service *for everyone*, we might not be fighting those endless wars in the first place. The first uses of conscription—forcing individuals to serve in the military—date back to the Roman era and to feudal times. The practice developed substantially during the Napoleonic era and spread quickly throughout Europe in the early years of the nineteenth century. In the US, conscription was first used by both the North and the South in the Civil War, and again in the Spanish-American War, World War I, World War II, the Korean War, and the Vietnam War. It was ended in the US in 1973. Since that time, America has relied on an all-volunteer military that it has used repeatedly, in at least ten major operations and dozens of lesser ones. As a result of the all-volunteer force and the lack of a requirement to serve, military issues and issues of war have all but completely faded from the American consciousness. Questions asked of voters in the 2018 election cycle indicated that an astounding 40 percent did not even know the US was still fighting in Afghanistan. The public is happy to let someone else fight the politicians' wars. It reveres the military but does not want to be a part of it. Surveys of eighteen- to twenty-nine-year-olds indicate that while a majority support the use of military forces to respond to various crises, only 15 percent have a willingness to serve in the military.[131] The burden of nearly two decades of wars around the world has been borne by approximately 1 percent of the population. It just seems morally wrong to ask such a small fraction of the population to place their lives at risk on behalf of the rest of us. While a return to conscription is politically highly unlikely, it should be seriously considered and debated. The "social contract" should require something of both parties, the government *and* its citizens.

Not only is it unfair for the public to depend on such a small segment of the population to fight its frequent wars, but it also puts a worrisome distance between the interests of the country and the loyalties of the armed forces. When the Roman Empire grew, the army could no longer be demobilized after a crisis, only to be remobilized at the next crisis. As a result, the government replaced the conscript army with an all-volunteer force. Because they expected recompense after their contracts ended, their loyalty was to their commanders, not to Rome.[132] This is not to imply that such is the case with our current military, but as a professional organization it must by necessity at least be concerned with, and act in ways to perpetuate, its continued existence.

So how do we fix the situation? One writer suggests that an annual reauthorization of the use of military force should be tied to the revival of the draft, the thinking being that if Congress failed to pass a new authorization, the draft would be reinstated.[133] For sure, such an arrangement would force this issue into the thinking of the public. The National Commission on Military, National, and Public Service, created by Congress in 2017, conducted a comprehensive review of such service. Among other things, they found what most of us already know: military service is a responsibility borne by few, public service needs an overhaul, and civic knowledge is lacking. No surprises there. They also found, however, that Americans are willing to consider a variety of options to encourage or require some form of service of all citizens. It remains to be seen if such support stands the test of time. The commission considered ways of requiring all citizens to serve, with varying ways to fulfill the requirement.[134] Unsurprisingly, in the end it stopped short of recommending a return to the military draft. It did, however, recognize the government's need for a method to organize the American people to provide for the common defense through mandatory military service, and it recommended that the US maintain a military draft mechanism for use in the event of national emergencies.

Conscription recently became a topic of renewed interest and concern with the US drone strike and killing of a top Iranian military official, followed by Iranian military retaliation and promise of further retribution. Draft-age men across the country expressed growing concern about a war in the Middle East that would require more troops than the all-volunteer force could provide.[135] While a revival of the draft remains highly unlikely, these events clearly demonstrate how quickly public opinion could be engaged to make a difference in the politicians' proclivity to war.

BUILDING OUR SYSTEMS TO AVOID WAR AS THE FIRST PRIORITY

The systems discussed earlier are complex and no doubt even adaptive in their behavior and must operate in highly chaotic and ambiguous environments. Their design, in some cases, defies true understanding, and our ability to test to a level at which we can trust they will work as designed and desired is problematic. The systems must be designed from the outset to prevent accidental war.

As we combine the people, processes, and technologies to form the command and control system, some things can be built in to limit immediate violent reactions. For example, in the case of ballistic missiles, before a missile launch is considered a threat, two phenomenologies must be employed to identify it: high-orbiting infrared satellites that detect the launch and its initial parameters and ground-based radars to refine the information about the potential target. There should be a similar requirement for units operating on the front lines and in high-tension areas, with time delays built in, and double checks on threatening behavior before a reaction is allowed. Automated responses should be allowed only in extreme time-critical situations in which the aggressive action of an adversary is certain. Defense against high-speed incoming missiles might be an example. Decisions to retaliate, while needing to be made promptly, require no such instantaneous response.

We must design extra "speed brakes" into command and control systems. In physics there is a concept called viscosity. Viscosity is the resistance of a fluid to the movement of neighboring portions relative to one another. It is a measure of opposition to flow or movement within the fluid. There is some value inherent in what could be called "bureaucratic viscosity," in which an attempt to speed a decision through the system, perhaps unnecessarily, is met with pushback from the system itself. Another physics, or electrical engineering, concept is the so-called RLC-circuit (resistor-inductor-capacitor). In such a circuit, the resistor functions to slow or throttle the flow of current, the capacitor allows charge to build up before letting it pass, creating a time delay, and an inductor serves to oppose slightly any changes in the rate of flow of the current. These three elements of a circuit combine to damp out electrical oscillations. They can overdamp and cause the oscillations to go away too quickly, they can underdamp and allow the oscillations to get out of control, or they can critically damp, so that the circuit operates at resonance. Analogies in the command and control systems would be built-in bottlenecks, information buildup, and time delays—brief, but sufficient to allow double checks against overreaction—and critical pushback against facile assumptions. In the case of tactical confrontations around the world, automated systems and sensors and the automated command and control systems directing them need to have similar requirements to double-check independent sources before responding. One of the tactical systems being considered for implementation is a weapon that automatically, using advanced AI techniques, returns fire when fired upon. There are great dangers to such knee-jerk behavior. Who fired? Is it the enemy or someone intending to provoke a fight? Are there innocents in the area? Processes and technologies will need to be inserted to answer these questions or to withhold response—or at least ensure that a human makes the decision.

Citizens must first be interested, then seek to understand the reasons for and the costs of war, and they must reject war as the first response to a crisis. Leaders must be willing to engage in meaningful discussions on how to limit war and its consequences. Weapons developers must design systems that employ all possible safeguards against knee-jerk behavior that could result in accidental, unintended conflict. There are ways to avoid war if we choose to do so. In all of the above, the operative action is to *choose*.

CONCLUSION

The world I have described is admittedly a scary one. It is more dangerous now than in recent memory, with heavily armed nations and groups and mercurial and militaristic leaders. Militaries are deployed with increasing frequency to locations around the globe and are equipped with frightening and growing arsenals of lethal weapons. Everything is connected to everything else, and the probability of an incident occurring and quickly escalating into global conflict is rising. We must find ways of lowering the pressure in the system. We must step back from the brink. To do so is possible, but it will require active interest and more effort by decision makers and the public.

Militaries are becoming more highly automated, with many decisions being turned over to machines. Numerous conditions and forces tempt nations and groups to go to war. Aggressive policies combined with high-technology weapons in the hands of militaries facing one another in high-pressure situations might cause us to stumble into a war. Citizens are strangely apathetic about such questions, while their governments demonstrate a stubborn proclivity to resort to war.

It could be argued that today is no different than any previous time. Many nations have historically expended large portions of their national treasure on weapons and have been enthralled by new weapons technologies. Colonial powers deployed their militaries widely, and sometimes brutally, throughout their empires. Rulers held grudges against other rulers and fought and threatened war for seemingly inconsequential reasons.

But things are qualitatively different now. Unlike the past, today's weapons are too complex to understand even by those who employ them. More concerning still is the fact that modern weapons and the decisions to use them are increasingly computer controlled, with human decision-making receding into the background and being replaced by automation. Unproven technologies incorporating artificial intelligence and autonomous behavior are being rushed into weapons and decision aids. On top of all of these trends is the fact that the world in general, and militaries in particular, are highly networked and tightly connected. Speed in all things has become the difference between failure and success in business or between victory and defeat on the battlefield. A growing number of automated tools are being employed to help us decide when and how to fight. We have to ensure that those automated tools are not taught our bad urges and that they do not merely continue our tendency to behave badly, albeit autonomously. The adoption—not necessarily the development—of new automated technologies for violence and military decision-making and command and control of forces will need to be measured and deliberate. We have to slow our rush to incorporate new technologies in warfare and ensure that automated command and control systems have built-in checks and balances to prevent accidental war.

The urges to war are many and have long been with us. Science and technology fascinate humans. From ancient and medieval times, science and magic were conflated. Technological achievements were considered sublime and looked upon reverentially. Inevitably, the attraction of new technologies found its way into the development of weapons for war. Americans, in particular, have long been transfixed by technology and superweapons, and for decades leaders have based US national security policy on a presumed technological superiority.

We are seduced by technology, and we are seduced by new weapons. We can't seem to get enough, fast enough. Advanced countries around the world, especially the US, spend vast sums on weapons that they are then tempted to use lest they go to waste.

The world remains plagued, as it has since ancient times, by nationalism and xenophobia and a willingness to perpetrate violence against others not like ourselves. Poorly educated citizens fall prey to rabid patriotism and appeals to exceptionalism, abetted by active government propaganda. World leaders exhibit antipathy toward science and cavalier disregard for facts and expertise. In recent years in the US, political leaders have undermined cooperative, science- and law-based approaches to solving complex problems and have shown disdain for, and active political antagonism toward, science and expert opinion. Governments around the world show a blatant disregard for facts and engage in active campaigns of disinformation to achieve political gains, at the expense of the safety of the people.

We are at a high risk of war because of our hyperconnectedness, made worse by an already too militaristic approach to foreign policy issues. National leaders have long shown a propensity to resort to military force, and recent ones have engaged in a battle of threats and counterthreats that raise the danger of confrontation. Nations and groups today are armed with both old-style and new automated weaponry, and antagonism and old hatreds run deep. Cyber and space warfare have emerged as new, unchartered forms of conflict that can quickly escalate. There are now far more chances for trouble and more chances for misunderstanding and miscalculation.

Nations we consider adversaries are well equipped and growing stronger, and we are facing them in hot spots around the world. The fact that others are gaining or even reaching parity frightens US leaders. We respond by deploying forces in too many places on too many questionable missions. The military is under enormous stress. High-tech weapons, inadequately tested and unproven, could make mistakes more likely. With a newly aggressive national security policy, we are adding pressure to an already pressurized system, throwing gas onto a smoldering fire. The dismantling of important institutions and the abrogation of arms control agreements create instability in foreign affairs. The global national security situation represents a state of unstable equilibrium in which a mistake or a small push could result in catastrophic reactions.

The absence of war may not constitute peace exactly, but it is certainly a prerequisite. Leaders talk about wanting to avoid war, but their actions often contradict their words. Citizens say they are against war, and politicians pledge to do all in their power to prevent it. Yet many of the actions of nations point toward war rather than peace. Decisions to go to war in the past were taken with great care and deliberation. Today, the resort to military force is almost commonplace. With new high-tech weaponry, leaders are lulled into unthinking behavior by the ease of going to war.

Citizens are capable of affecting change but do not. They are complacent. While political, social, and economic factors play an important role, it stands to reason that if citizens better understood the costs of war to themselves, let alone future generations, they would be better equipped and might be more willing to push back against the rush to military force. Long after conflicts have ended, the effects of war on soldiers and their families and on the civilian population in the countries where they are fought are devastating. The public needs to understand that the costs are enormous, most importantly in personal terms, but in financial terms as well: American citizens or their children will end up paying them. Unfortunately, these costs are currently hidden or obfuscated. The average citizen has no stake in the nation's military adventures and as a result rarely questions the frequent decisions by politicians to resort to force.

The public must start paying attention. We can get its attention by pushing back against the constant drumbeat of prowar war narratives, by changing the conversation and ensuring that citizens hear both sides of the arguments about war. Scholars, authors, entertainers, and other influential individuals and groups have to emerge and demand to be heard. They must speak to all citizens, especially the younger generation who will inevitably become our future leaders. An informed public must then demand policy, legal, and institutional changes that will reduce the chances of unwanted and unnecessary wars.

We must get over our thinking that we can go it alone and that our enormous investments in weapons will ensure our continued dominance. We must reaffirm commitments to and from our allies. While we may remain ahead in some or most areas, other countries have increasingly powerful voices. We have to re-embrace arms control negotiations as a way to lower the chances of war. We can take a leadership role and engage other nations, peer adversaries and developing nations alike, to consider international agreements limiting and controlling some weapons applications. We must be open to negotiations, to the development of treaties or agreements-short-of-treaties with China, Russia, and other highly armed countries. We must find ways to limit the proliferation of hypersonic weapons, cyber weapons, space weapons, and those containing problematic applications of artificial intelligence. We have to reemphasize arms control solutions.

In such a high-speed, high-pressure international environment, it is more important now than ever that citizens join in any debate about the use of armed force. The public should demand that its representatives take a position on military operations and insist on an authorization to use military force whenever the executive considers deploying US forces. Each new deployment above a certain size must be separately authorized and funded—no more fighting wars on a credit card. Government leaders must better inform citizens of the costs and benefits of military deployments. If we are to go to war, individual citizens must be asked to participate. Conscription and national service should be considered. These would ensure that the public had an interest in minimizing the use of US forces in unnecessary wars. Finally, weapon systems must incorporate safeguards against dangerous applications of machine decision-making.

If the recent, devastating COVID-19 pandemic has taught us anything, it is that, in a highly interconnected and globalized world, shocks travel fast. Globalization is a fact. Nations must depend on one another. Aggression and military posturing seem jarringly out of place when large numbers of citizens in all countries are succumbing to the violence of a natural killer. Coordinated, collaborative actions—not mistrust and old antagonisms—will be the key to mitigating the effects of future crises.

"Nothing in history is inevitable, including the probable," said Reinhold Niebuhr. "So long as war has not broken out, we still have the possibility of avoiding it."[1]

NOTES

PREFACE

1. Marinus Ossewaarde, "Crises of Modernity Discourses and the Rise of Financial Technologies in a Contested Mechanized World," *Philosophy and Technology*, no. 31 (2018): 60.

2. Michael A. Cacciatore, Haley Madden, Molly J. Simis, and Sara K. Yeo, "The Lure of Rationality: Why Does the Deficit Model Persist in Science Communication?," *Public Understanding of Science* 25, no. 4 (2016): 402.

INTRODUCTION

1. Melissa Girard, "How Autocratic Our Country Is Becoming: The Sentimental Poetess at War," *Journal of Modern Literature* 32, no. 2 (2009): 59.

2. Lawrence Sondhaus, "Civilian and Military Power," *International Encyclopedia of the First World War*, August 25, 2015, https://encyclopedia.1914-1918-online.net/article/civilian_and_military_power.

3. Robert Weldon Whalen, "War Losses (Germany)," *International Encyclopedia of the First World War*, October 8, 2014, https://encyclopedia.1914-1918-online.net/article/war_losses_germany.

4. Chris Hedges, "What Every Person Should Know about War," *New York Times*, July 6, 2003.

5. Watson Institute, "Costs of War," Brown University, accessed September 9, 2019, https://watson.brown.edu/costsofwar/.

6. John Arquilla, "The Big Kill," *Foreign Policy*, December 3, 2012.

7. John Gray, "Steven Pinker Is Wrong about Violence and War," *The Guardian*, March 13, 2015.

8. Dylan Thomas Farley, "Objects in Mirror Are Closer Than They Appear," *Real Clear Defense*, October 15, 2019.

9. Richard English, *Modern War: A Very Short Introduction* (Oxford: Oxford University Press, 2013), 6.

10. Ibid., 8.

11. Sean M. Lynn-Jones, "Offense-Defense Theory and Its Critics," *Security Studies* 4, no. 4 (Summer 1995): 667.

12. Daniel R. Lake, "Technology, Qualitative Superiority, and the Overstretched American Military," *Strategic Studies Quarterly* 6, no. 4 (Winter 2012): 75.

13. Ray Furlong, "The Changing Story of Russia's 'Little Green Men' Invasion," Radio Free Europe, February 25, 2019, www.rferl.org/a/russia-ukraine-crimea/29790037.html.

14. Zachery Tyson Brown, "Unmasking War's Changing Character," Modern War Institute, March 12, 2019, https://mwi.usma.edu/unmasking-wars-changing-character/.

15. Michael Beschloss, *Presidents of War* (New York: Crown, 2018), 19.

16. Jacquelyn Schneider, *Digitally-Enabled Warfare: The Capability-Vulnerability Paradox* (Washington, DC: Center for a New American Security, 2016), 4.

ONE. A GIANT ARMED NERVOUS SYSTEM

1. Patrick Tucker, "The Future the U.S. Military Is Constructing: A Giant Armed Nervous System," *Defense One*, September 26, 2017, www.defenseone.com/technology/2017/09/future-us-military-constructing-giant-armed-nervous-system/141303/.

2. Daniel Brown and Skye Gould, "The U.S. Has 1.3 Million Troops Stationed around the World—Here Are the Major Hotspots," Business Insider, August 31, 2017; W. J. Hennigan, "Inside the New American Way of War," *Time*, December 11, 2017, 46.

3. David Vine, "Where in the World Is the U.S. Military?," *Politico*, July/August 2015.

4. Kristin Bialik, "U.S. Active Duty Military Presence Overseas Is at Its Smallest in Decades," Pew Research Center, August 22, 2017, www.pewresearch

.org/fact-tank/2017/08/22/u-s-active-duty-military-presence-overseas
-is-at-its-smallest-in-decades/.

5. GovLoop, *The Joint Information Environment* (Washington, DC, 2014), 7, www.govloop.com/wp-content/uploads/2014/10/JIE_Guide_FINAL.pdf.

6. Mark Pomerleau and Mike Gruss, "Army Budget Request Adds $1.5B for Network Modernization, *C4ISRNET*, April 18, 2019, www.c4isrnet.com /it-networks/2019/04/18/army-budget-request-adds-15b-for-network -modernization/.

7. Tucker, "Future the U.S. Military Is Constructing."

8. Charles Pope, "Goldfein Details Air Force's Move toward a 'Fully Networked,' Multi-domain Future," US Air Force website, September 17, 2019, www.af.mil/News/Article-Display/Article/1963310/goldfein-details-air -forces-move-toward-a-fully-networked-multi-domain-future/.

9. Robert R. Leonhard, Thomas H. Buchanan, James L. Hillman, John M. Nolen, and Timothy J. Galpin, "A Concept for Command and Control," *Johns Hopkins APL Technical Digest* 23, no. 2 (2010): 159.

10. Daniel M. West and John R. Allen, "How Artificial Intelligence Is Transforming the World," Brookings Institution, April 24, 2018, www.brook ings.edu/research/how-artificial-intelligence-is-transforming-the-world/.

11. Zachary S. Davis, *Artificial Intelligence on the Battlefield* (Livermore, CA: Lawrence Livermore National Laboratory, March 2019), 10.

12. Michael T. Klare, "The US Military Is Preparing for a New War," *The Nation*, June 5, 2019.

13. Zac Rogers, "Have Strategists Drunk the 'AI Race' Kool Aid?," *War on the Rocks*, June 4, 2019, https://warontherocks.com/2019/06/have-strategists -drunk-the-ai-race-kool-aid/.

14. Elsa B. Kania, "Minds at War: China's Pursuit of Military Advantage through Cognitive Science and Biotechnology," *Prism* 8, no. 3 (January 2020): 85.

15. United Nations Department of Economic and Social Affairs, *2018 Revision of World Urbanization Prospects* (New York: United Nations, May 26, 2018), 5.

16. Robert N. Townsend, "Tactical Automation on the Battlefield: Who Is in Control?" (master's thesis, US Army Command and General Staff College, 1992), 8.

17. National Research Council. *Realizing the Potential of C4I: Fundamental Challenges* (Washington, DC: National Academies Press, 1999), 27.

18. Callum Roberts, "Just How Smart Is an Octopus?," *Washington Post*, January 6, 2017.

19. Amanda Gibbs, "Cephalopod Encephalization," *Eukaryon* 13 (2017): 49.

20. Michelle Starr, "Octopus Arms Are Capable of Making Decisions without Input from Their Brains," *Science Alert*, June 26, 2019, www.science alert.com/here-s-how-octopus-arms-make-decisions-without-input-from -the-brain.

21. Frank W. Grasso, "The Octopus with Two Brains: How Are Distributed and Central Representations Integrated in the Octopus Central Nervous System?," in *Cephalopod Cognition*, ed. Anne-Sophie Darmaillacq, Ludovic Dickel, and Jennifer Mather (Cambridge: Cambridge University Press, 2014), 94–122.

22. Peter Godfrey-Smith, *Other Minds: The Octopus, the Sea, and the Deep Origins of Consciousness* (New York: Farrar, Strauss, and Giroux, 2016), 105.

23. Ibid., 98.

24. Claudius Aelianus, *On the Characteristics of Animals*, trans. A. F. Schofield (Cambridge, MA: Loeb Classical Library, 1959), 87, quoted in Godfrey-Smith, *Other Minds*, 43.

25. J. Garrett Sullivan, "Knowledge of Graduates of the Watch Officer/ Watch Chief Course," OTS Master's Level Projects and Papers, Old Dominion University, 2011, 13, https://digitalcommons.odu.edu/cgi/viewcontent.cgi? article=1016&context=ots_masters_projects.

26. Stanley Kubrick, dir., *2001: A Space Odyssey* (Metro-Goldwyn-Mayer Corp., 1968).

27. Federico Clemente and Stephen Gray, "The Future of the Command Post," *Cyber Edge*, October 1, 2018, www.afcea.org/content/future-command -post.

28. See Z. M. L.," Living Well in the Technosocial World: A review of Shannon Vallor's *Technology and the Virtues*," *Librarian Shipwreck*, August 24, 2017, https://wp.me/p38S12-EF, and Benjamin I. Huff, Randolph-Macon College, review of *Technology and the Virtues: A Philosophical Guide to a Future Worth Wanting*, by Shannon Vallor, *Notre Dame Philosophical Reviews*, April 20, 2017, https://ndpr.nd.edu/news/technology-and-the-virtues-a-philosophical -guide-to-a-future-worth-wanting/.

29. Peter J. Denning and Ted G. Lewis, "Intelligence May Not Be Computable," *American Scientist* 107, no. 6 (2019): 349.

30. Robert K. Ackerman, "AI Will Reboot the Army's Battlefield," *Signal Magazine*, September 2018, www.afcea.org/content/ai-will-reboot-armys -battlefield.

31. Alexander Kott and Dave S. Alberts, "How Do You Command an Army of Intelligent Things?," *IEEE Computer*, no. 12 (2017): 96.

32. Kelsey D. Atherton, "Can the Army Perfect an AI Strategy for a Fast and Deadly Future?," *C4ISRNET*, October 15, 2019, www.c4isrnet.com

/artificial-intelligence/2019/10/15/can-the-army-perfect-an-ai-strategy-for-a-fast-and-deadly-future/.

33. "Teaching AI Systems to Adapt to Dynamic Environments," Defense Advanced Research Projects Agency, February 14, 2019, www.darpa.mil/news-events/2019-02-14.

34. "Verbatim," *Air Force Magazine*, January/February 2020, 32.

35. Patrick Tucker, "Report: Weapons AI Increasingly Replacing, Not Augmenting, Human Decision-Making," *Defense One*, September 26, 2016.

36. Matt Turek, "Explainable Artificial Intelligence (XAI)," Defense Advanced Research Projects Agency, n.d., accessed May 6, 2020, www.darpa.mil/program/explainable-artificial-intelligence.

37. Kimberly Underwood, "Artificial Intelligence Use in Command and Control," *Signal Magazine*, May 17, 2018.

38. Sydney J. Freedberg Jr., "Why A 'Human in The Loop' Can't Control AI: Richard Danzig," *Breaking Defense*, June 1, 2018.

39. Andy J. Fawkes and Martin Menzel, "The Future Role of Artificial Intelligence: Military Opportunities and Challenges," *Journal of the Joint Airpower Competence Center* 27 (2018): 76.

40. "Teaching A.I Systems."

41. BEC Crew, "Google's AI Has Learned to Become Highly Aggressive in Stressful Situations," *Science Alert*, March 31, 2018.

42. Mark Pomerleau, "Top Intel Official Warns of Bias in Military Algorithms," *C4ISRNET*, November 18, 2020, www.c4isrnet.com/artificial-intelligence/2020/11/18/top-intel-official-warns-of-bias-in-military-algorithms/.

43. Spencer Ackerman, "If Israel Bombs Iran, It'll Jam, Spoof and Hack First," *Wired*, November 17, 2011.

44. Jeremy Bender, "Russia May Still Have an Automated Nuclear Launch System Aimed across the Northern Hemisphere," *Business Insider*, September 4, 2014.

45. Stephen I. Schwartz, *Atomic Audit: The Costs and Consequences of U.S. Nuclear Weapons since 1940* (Washington, DC: Brookings Institution Press, 1988), 209.

46. Adam Lowther and Curtis McGiffin, "America Needs a 'Dead Hand,'" *War on the Rocks*, August 16, 2019, https://warontherocks.com/2019/08/america-needs-a-dead-hand/.

47. Sydney J. Freedberg Jr., "No AI for Nuclear Command and Control: JAIC's Shanahan," *Breaking Defense*, September 25, 2019.

48. Christopher Paul, Colin P. Clarke, Bonnie L. Triezenberg, David Manheim, and Bradley Wilson, *Improving C2 and Situational Awareness for*

Operations in and through the Information Environment (Santa Monica, CA: RAND Corporation, 2018), 99.

49. Kristina Lindborg, "Hypersonic Missiles May Be Unstoppable. Is Society Ready?," *Christian Science Monitor*, March 31, 2020.

50. Ben Dickson, "Inside DARPA's Effort to Create Explainable Artificial Intelligence," *Tech Talks*, January 10, 2019, https://bdtechtalks.com/2019/01 /10/darpa-xai-explainable-artificial-intelligence/; David Gunning, "Explainable Artificial Intelligence (XAI)," *DARPA Program Update*, November 2017, www.documentcloud.org/documents/5794867-National-Security-Archive -David-Gunning-DARPA.html.

51. Theresa Hitchens, "DOD Should Consider Truly Autonomous Weapons: Bipartisan AI Commission," *Breaking Defense*, November 5, 2019.

52. Aaron Boyd, "White House Tech Chief Calls Europe's AI Principles Clumsy Compared to U.S. Approach," *Nextgov*, February 20, 2020, www.next gov.com/cio-briefing/2020/02/white-house-tech-chief-calls-europes-ai -principles-clumsy-compared-us-approach/163241/.

53. Joe Hayes, email to author, February 1, 2019.

54. Zachery Tyson Brown, "Unmasking War's Changing Character," Modern War Institute, March 12, 2019, https://mwi.usma.edu/unmasking-wars -changing-character/.

55. Richard Danzig, *Technology Roulette* (Washington, DC: Center for a New American Security, June 2018), 9.

56. Hannah Ritchie and Max Roser, "Technology Adoption," n.d., accessed December 5, 2019, https://ourworldindata.org/technology-adoption.

57. Harvey M. Sapolsky and Jeremy Shapiro, "Casualties, Technology, and America's Future Wars," *Parameters, U.S. Army War College Quarterly* 26, no. 2 (1996): 119, www.google.com/books/edition/Parameters/2UgGfNz RwjcC?hl=en&gbpv=1&dq=sapolsky+shapiro++parameters,+us+army+war +college+quarterly+volume+26,+no+2&pg=PA1&printsec=frontcover.

TWO. URGES TO VIOLENCE

1. Perry Miller, *The Life of the Mind in America* (New York: Harcourt, Brace and World, 1963), 276.

2. David E. Nye, *American Technological Sublime* (Cambridge, MA: MIT Press, 1994), xix.

3. L. M. Sacasas, "American Technological Sublime: Our Civil Religion," *The Frailest Thing* (blog), October 21, 2011, https://thefrailestthing.com/2011 /10/21/american-technological-sublime-our-civil-religion/.

4. Edmund Burke, *Philosophical Inquiry into the Origin of Our Ideas of the Sublime and Beautiful* (Baltimore: William and Joseph Neal, 1833), 44; Kyle Craft-Jenkins, "Artificial Intelligence and the Technological Sublime: How Virtual Characters Influence the Landscape of Modern Sublimity" (master's thesis, University of Kentucky, 2012), 9.

5. Nina A. Kollars, "By the Seat of Their Pants: Military Technological Adaptation in War" (PhD diss., Ohio State University, 2012), 16.

6. H. Bruce Franklin, *War Stars: The Superweapon and the American Imagination* (Amherst: University of Massachusetts Press, 2008), 20.

7. Stanley Waterloo, *Armageddon: A Tale of Love, War, and Invention* (Chicago: Rand McNally, 1898), 258, quoted in Franklin, *War Stars*, 170.

8. John M. Ashbrook, "Why We Need Military Superiority," unnumbered chapter in *No Left Turns: A Handbook for Conservatives Based on the Writings of John M. Ashbrook* (Fairfield, OH: Hamilton Hobby Press, 1986), https://ashbrook.org/programs/citizens/publications/books/no-left-turns -contents/why-military-superiority/.

9. "Reagan Proposes Star Wars Missile Defense System," *New York Times*, March 23, 1983.

10. Defense Science Board, *The Report of the Defense Science Board Task Force on the National Aero-Space Plane* (Washington, DC: Department of Defense, November 1992), 25.

11. Chris B. Petty, "Reagan's Impossible Dream: The X-30 National Aerospace Plane," *High Frontier*, January 2, 2016.

12. Victor Davis Hanson, "Military Technology and American Culture," *New Atlantis*, no. 1 (Spring 2003): 36.

13. Drew Gilpin Faust, "Telling War Stories: Reflections of a Civil War Historian," (2011 Jefferson Lecture in the Humanities, Washington, DC, May 2, 2011), quoted in Jennifer Howard, "In Jefferson Lecture, Drew Faust Traces the Fascination of War, from Homer to Bin Laden," *Chronicle of Higher Education*, May 2, 2011.

14. Arthur C. Clarke, *Profiles of the Future: An Inquiry into the Limits of the Possible* (London: Pan Books, 1973), 39.

15. Johann Wolfgang von Goethe, "The Sorcerer's Apprentice," 1797, https://germanstories.vcu.edu/goethe/zauber_e4.html.

16. E. F. Beall, "Hesiod's Prometheus and the Devil in Myth," *Journal of the History of Ideas* 52, no. 3 (July–September 1991): 364; Hesiod, *Theogony and Works and Days*, trans. Catherine M. Schlegel and Henry Weinfield (Ann Arbor: University of Michigan Press, 2009), 59. The original Greek should properly be translated as "jar," rather than the more common "box."

17. Henry Brooks Adams to Charles Francis Adams Jr., April 11, 1862, in *A Cycle of Adams Letters*, ed. William Chauncey Ford (London: Constable, 1921), 135, quoted in Cynthia Wachtell, *War No More* (Baton Rouge: Louisiana State University Press, 2010), 135.

18. National Intelligence Council, *Global Trends: Paradox of Progress* (Washington, DC: Office of the Director of National Intelligence, January 2017), 6.

19. Sharon Tregaskis, "Cut and Paste," *Notre Dame Magazine*, Spring 2018, 23.

20. Jacob Bronowski, *Science and Human Values* (New York: Harper and Row, 1965), 70–71.

21. Albert Camus, "Banquet Speech," Nobel Prize in Literature, 1957, www.nobelprize.org/prizes/literature/1957/camus/speech/ .

22. Isaiah Berlin, *Four Essays on Liberty* (Oxford: Oxford University Press, 1969), 170.

23. Michael Wiescher, "Arthur E. Haas, His Life and Colleagues," *Physics in Perspective* 19 (2017): 48.

24. Albert Speer, "Final Statement of Albert Speer," *Traces of War*, July 1, 2016, www.tracesofwar.com/articles/4573/Final-statement-Albert-Speer.htm.

25. Center for Responsive Politics, "Annual Lobbying on Defense," Opensecrets.org, accessed March 19, 2019, www.opensecrets.org/federal-lobbying/sectors/summary?id=D.

26. "Aerospace and Defense Year in Review and 2018 Forecast," Price Waterhouse Cooper, June 1, 2018, www.defense-aerospace.com/articles-view/release/3/193626/pwc-reviews-aerospace-and-defense-industry-2017.html.

27. Scott Thompson, "Aerospace and Defense Industry Hits Record Revenues and Profits in 2018," Price Waterhouse Cooper, May 16, 2019, www.pwc.com/us/en/industries/industrial-products/industrial-insights/aerospace-and-defense-industry-record-revenues-profits-2018.html.

28. Amanda Macias, "Here's How Much the CEOs of America's Top Defense Companies Are Paid," CNBC, March 8, 2018.

29. David Cortright, *Peace: A History of Movements and Ideas* (Cambridge: Cambridge University Press, 2008), 99.

30. John T. Correll, "Eisenhower's Farewell Warning," *Air Force Magazine*, August 2018.

31. Andrew Bacevich, "The Tyranny of Defense Inc," *The Atlantic*, January/February 2011.

32. Jonathan D. Caverley, *Democratic Militarism* (Cambridge: Cambridge University Press, 2014), 119.

33. Ibid., 257.

34. Louis Uchitelle, "The U.S. Still Leans on the Military-Industrial Complex," *New York Times*, September 22, 2017.

35. Casey Borch and Michael Wallace, "Military Spending and Economic Well-Being in the American States: The Post-Vietnam Era," *Social Forces* 88, no. 4 (2010): 1729.

36. Jonathan Grant, "'Merchants of Death': The International Traffic in Arms," *Origins* 6, no. 3 (December 2012), https://origins.osu.edu/article/merchants-death-international-traffic-arms.

37. Sissela Bok, *A Strategy for Peace* (New York: Pantheon Books, 1989), 31.

38. John Eppstein, *The Catholic Tradition of the Law of Nations* (Washington, DC: Catholic Association for International Peace, 1935), 132; James Turner Johnson, *Just War Tradition and the Restraint of War* (Princeton, NJ: Princeton University Press, 1981), 340.

39. Cortright, *Peace*, 41. See also John Mack, "Nicholas II and the 'Rescript for Peace' of 1898: Apostle of Peace or Shrewd Politician?," *Russian History* 31, nos. 1/2 (2004): 84.

40. George C. Marshall, Nobel Peace Prize Acceptance Speech, December 11, 1953, www.nobelprize.org/prizes/peace/1953/marshall/acceptance-speech/.

41. Michael T. Klare, "How Resource Scarcity and Climate Change Could Produce a Global Explosion," *The Nation*, April 22, 2013.

42. Office of the Director of National Intelligence, "DNI Coats Opening Statement on the 2019 Worldwide Threat Assessment of the U.S. Intelligence Community," January 29, 2019, www.dni.gov/index.php/newsroom/congressional-testimonies/item/1949-dni-coats-opening-statement-on-the-2019-worldwide-threat-assessment-of-the-us-intelligence-community.

43. John Vandiver, "Strategy Prepares Army Special Ops for Future Battles," *Stars and Stripes*, October 25, 2019.

44. Center for Naval Analysis, *National Security and the Threat of Climate Change* (Alexandria, VA: CNA, 2007). See also James Stavridis, "National Security Risks Are Rising with Sea Levels," Bloomberg, May 13, 2019.

45. Klare, "How Resource Scarcity."

46. Johnson, *Just War Tradition*, 236.

47. "The Thirty Years' War," History, August 21, 2018, www.history.com/topics/reformation/thirty-years-war.

48. "Marching on Their Stomachs," review of *The Taste of War*, by Lizie Collingham, *The Economist*, February 5, 2011.

49. Norman Myers, "Environmental Refugees: An Emergent Security Issue," paper presented at the 13th Economic Forum, May 22, 2005, http://probeinternational.org/library/wp-content/uploads/2011/04/14851.pdf.

50. Jeffrey Mazo, "Chapter Three: Darfur: The First Modern Climate-Change Conflict," *Adelphi Papers* 49, no. 409 (2009): 73.

51. Hannah Brock, *Competition over Resources: Drivers of Insecurity and the Global South* (London: Oxford Research Group, 2011), 12.

52. UN Interagency Framework Team for Preventive Action, *Renewable Resources and Conflict* (New York: United Nations, 2012), 14.

53. Albert Breton and Margot Breton, "Nationalism Revisited," in *Nationalism and Rationality*, ed. Albert Breton, Gianluigi Galeotti, Pierre Salmon, and Ronald Wintrobe (London: Cambridge University Press, 1995), 111.

54. Cortright, *Peace*, 44.

55. Susan L. Carruthers, *The Media at War* (London: Red Globe Press, 2011), 64.

56. Florian Bieber, "Is Nationalism on the Rise? Assessing Global Trends," *Ethnopolitics* 17, no. 5 (2018): 530.

57. Anthony Everitt, *Cicero: The Life and Times of Rome's Greatest Politician* (New York: Random House, 2001), 34.

58. Richard English, *Modern War: A Very Short Introduction* (Oxford: Oxford University Press, 2013), 37.

59. Bertrand Russell, "The Next Half-Century," in *The Basic Writings of Bertrand Russell*, ed. Robert E. Egner and Lester E. Denonn (London: Routledge, 2009), 690.

60. John Schaar, "What Is Patriotism," *The Nation*, July 15, 1991.

61. Jane Addams, *Newer Ideals of Peace* (New York: Macmillan, 1907), 211.

62. Reinhold Niebuhr, *Moral Man and Immoral Society* (Louisville, KY: Westminster John Knox Press, 2001), 91.

63. Gary R. Jahn, "Patriotism and the Military in Tolstoy's Philosophy: Reflections and Refractions," in *Literature and War: Reflections and Refractions*, ed. E. W. Trahan (Monterey, CA: Monterey Institute of International Studies, 1985), 117.

64. Richard A. Cloward and Frances Fox Piven, "What Is Patriotism," *The Nation*, July 15, 1991.

65. Carruthers, *Media at War*, 9.

66. Sean Aday, "The US Media, Foreign Policy, and Public Support for War," in *The Oxford Handbook of Political Communication*, ed. Kate Kenski and Kathleen Hall Jamieson (Oxford: Oxford University Press, 2018), 316.

67. Philip Seib, "Effects of Real-Time News Coverage on Foreign Policy," *Journal of Conflict Studies* 20, no. 2 (2000), https://journals.lib.unb.ca/index.php/JCS/article/view/4309.

68. Tim Allen, "Perceiving Contemporary Wars," in *The Media of Conflict*, ed. Tim Allen and Jean Seaton (New York: Zed Books, 1999), 37.

69. Danielle Page, "The Science behind Why We Can't Look Away from Tragedy," NBC News, September 28, 2017.

70. Catharine Savage Brosman, "The Functions of War Literature," *South Central Review* 9, no. 1 (Spring 1992): 95.

71. Thomas Rid, "Think Again: Cyberwar," *Foreign Policy*, February 27, 2012, https://foreignpolicy.com/2012/02/27/think-again-cyberwar/.

72. Robin Andersen and Tanner Mirrlees, "Media, Technology, and the Culture of Militarism: Watching, Playing, and Resisting the War Society," *Democratic Communique* 26, no. 2 (Fall 2014): 8.

73. Ibid., 2.

74. David Shribman, "What's Wrong with Experts?," *Notre Dame Magazine*, Winter 2019–20, 26.

75. Isaac Asimov, "A Cult of Ignorance," *Newsweek*, January 21, 1980.

76. Tom Nichols, *The Death of Expertise* (New York: Oxford University Press, 2017), 5.

77. Richard Hofstadter, *Anti-intellectualism in American Life* (New York: Vintage Books, 1962), 38.

78. Charles Levinson, "Under Trump, Expert Advisory Panels on the Decline," Reuters, July 30, 2019; Robert Gebelhoff, "Trump Isn't Even Hiding His Disdain for Science Anymore," *Washington Post*, October 23, 2019.

79. Russell Muirhead and Nancy L. Rosenblum, *A Lot of People Are Saying* (Princeton, NJ: Princeton University Press, 2019), 11.

80. Jonathan Swift, "Contributions to the Examiner," in *The Prose Works of Jonathan Swift,* vol. 9, ed. Temple Scott (London: George Bell and Sons, 1902), 82. See also Robinson Meyer, "The Grim Conclusions of the Largest-Ever Study of Fake News," *The Atlantic*, March 8, 2018.

81. Joseph Foley, "10 Deepfake Examples That Terrified and Amused the Internet," *Creative Bloq*, March 23, 2020, www.creativebloq.com/features/deepfake-examples.

82. Office of the Director of National Intelligence, "DNI Coats Opening Statement."

83. Daniel Benjamin and Steven Simon, "How Fake News Could Lead to Real War," *Politico*, July 5, 2019.

84. Joe Hayes, email to author, February 1, 2018.

85. Sisela Bok, *Lying: Moral Choice in Public and Private Life* (New York: Vintage Books, 1999), 18.

86. Hannah Arendt, *The Origins of Totalitarianism* (New York: Harcourt, 196), 382.

87. Hannah Arendt, *Between Past and Future* (New York: Penguin Books, 2006), 257.

88. Seymour Martin Lipset, *Political Man: The Social Bases of Politics* (Baltimore: Johns Hopkins University Press, 1981), 101.

89. Moses Shayo, "Education, Militarism and Civil Wars," unpublished paper, Hebrew University of Jerusalem Department of Economics, July 2008, https://pluto.mscc.huji.ac.il/~mshayo/Education_and_Militarism.pdf.

90. Caverley, *Democratic Militarism*, 75.

91. Gudrun Østby, Henrik Urdal, and Kendra Dupuy, "Does Education Lead to Pacification? A Systematic Review of Statistical Studies on Education and Political Violence," *Review of Educational Research*, Peace Research Institute Oslo 89, no. 1 (2019): 80.

92. Mikael Hjerm, "Education, Xenophobia, and Nationalism: A Comparative Analysis," *Journal of Ethnic and Migration Studies* 27, no. 1 (2001): 56. The countries ranged from Australia and Canada to the Czech Republic and Hungary.

93. Thucydides, *History of the Peloponnesian War*, trans. Rex Warner (New York: Penguin Books, 1972), 213.

94. Marshall, Nobel Peace Prize Acceptance Speech.

THREE. STUMBLING INTO WAR

1. Sebastien Roblin, "A War Begins: How Iran Shot Down a U.S. RQ-4N Surveillance Drone," *National Interest*, June 21, 2019.

2. Jonathan Marcus, "Could an Ancient Greek Have Predicted a U.S. China Conflict?," BBC News, March 25, 2019.

3. Graham Allison, "The Thucydides Trap: Are the U.S. and China Headed for War?," *The Atlantic*, September 24, 2015.

4. "Technology Quarterly: A New Revolution: Technological Progress in China Could Still Lead to Fireworks," *The Economist*, January 2, 2020.

5. Leon Whyte, "The Real Thucydides Trap," *The Diplomat*, May 6, 2015.

6. David Meyer, "Vladimir Putin Says Whoever Leads in Artificial Intelligence Will Rule the World," *Fortune*, September 4, 2017.

7. National Intelligence Council, *Assessing Russian Activities and Intentions in Recent U.S. Elections* (Washington, DC: Office of the Director of National Intelligence, January 6, 2017), 1.

8. Brian Naylor, "Russia Hacked U.S. Power Grid—So What Will the Trump Administration Do about It?," NPR, March 23, 2018.

9. Daniel Brown, "Russia Says It Has Deployed Its Uran-9 Robotic Tank to Syria—Here's What It Can Do," Business Insider, May 15, 2018.

10. Foreign Policy Association, "China and America: The New Geopolitical Equation," *Great Decisions (Update)*, Spring 2018, 2.

11. Joseph Marks, "The Cybersecurity 202: U.S. Officials: It's China Hacking That Keeps Us Up at Night," *Washington Post*, March 6, 2019.

12. Commission on the Theft of American Intellectual Property, *The Report of the Commission on the Theft of American Intellectual Property (Update)* (Washington, DC: National Bureau of Asian Research, 2017), 1.

13. Michelle Nichols, "North Korea Took $2 Billion in Cyberattacks to Fund Weapons Program: U.N. Report," Reuters, August 5, 2019.

14. Center for Global Security Research, *Multi-domain Strategic Competition: Rewards and Risks* (Livermore, CA: Lawrence Livermore National Laboratory, December 2018), 7.

15. Ryan Pickrell, "The US Has Been Getting 'Its Ass Handed to It' in War Games Simulating Fights against Russia and China," Business Insider, March 8, 2019.

16. Union of Concerned Scientists, *UCS Satellite Database*, accessed December 16, 2019, www.ucsusa.org/resources/satellite-database.

17. Anatoly Zak, *Russian Military and Dual-Purpose Spacecraft: Latest Status and Operational Overview* (Washington, DC: CNA Corporation, June 2019), 1.

18. David Montgomery, "A New Hope," *Washington Post Magazine*, December 8, 2019, 19.

19. Mark Rice, "NATO's New Order: The Alliance after the Cold War," *Origins* 9, no. 7 (April 2016), https://origins.osu.edu/article/natos-new-order-alliance-after-cold-war.

20. Andrew E. Kramer, "Russia Calls New U.S. Missile Defense System a Direct Threat," *New York Times*, May 12, 2016.

21. Nicu Popescu and Stanislav Secrieru, *Hacks Leaks and Disruptions: Russian Cyber Strategies* (Paris: EU Institute for Security Studies, 2018), 5.

22. "Special Report on NATO at 70," *The Economist*, March 16, 2019, 6; Ilya Arkhipov and Marek Strzelecki, "Putin Warns NATO Missile Shield Is a Threat to Peace in Europe," Bloomberg News, May 13, 2016.

23. Robert E. Hamilton, "Able Archer at 35: Lessons of the 1983 War Scare," Foreign Policy Research Institute, December 3, 2018, www.fpri.org/article/2018/12/able-archer-at-35-lessons-of-the-1983-war-scare/.

24. David Brennan, "Iranian Navy Accidentally Fires on Own Ship in Training Exercise Gone Wrong," *Newsweek*, May 11, 2020.

25. Barbara Salazar Torreon and Sofia Plagakis, *Instances of Use of United States Armed Forces Abroad, 1798–2019* (Washington, DC: Congressional Research Service, January 13, 2020).

26. Lawrence A. Yates, *Global War on Terrorism Occasional Paper 15. The U.S. Military's Experience in Stability Operations, 1789–2005* (Fort Leavenworth, KS: Combat Studies Institute Press, 2006), 2.

27. Stephen Losey, "Fewer Planes Are Ready to Fly: Air Force Mission-Capable Rates Decline amid Pilot Crisis," *Air Force Times*, March 5, 2018; Brian W. Everstine, "Breaking Down USAF's 70-Percent Overall Mission Capable Rate," *Air Force Magazine*, May 19, 2020.

28. Robert Faturechi, Megan Rose, and T. Christian Miller, "Years of Warnings, Then Death and Disaster: How the Navy Failed Its Sailors," ProPublica, February 7, 2019, https://features.propublica.org/navy-accidents/us-navy-crashes-japan-cause-mccain/.

29. Lolita C. Baldor, "Mattis: Dire Impact on Military without Stable Budget," AP News, February 6, 2018.

30. Megan Eckstein, "Navy Reverting DDGs Back to Physical Throttles, after Fleet Rejects Touchscreen Controls," U.S. Naval Institute News, August 9, 2019, https://news.usni.org/2019/08/09/navy-reverting-ddgs-back-to-physical-throttles-after-fleet-rejects-touchscreen-controls.

31. Hennigan, "Inside the New American Way."

32. Bertrand Russell, "The Next Half-Century," in *The Basic Writings of Bertrand Russell*, ed. Robert E. Egner and Lester E. Denonn (London: Routledge, 2009), 658.

33. Tim Sweijs and Floris Holstege, *Threats, Arms and Conflicts: Taking Stock of Interstate Military Competition in Today's World* (The Hague, NL: The Hague Center for Strategic Studies, December 6, 2018).

34. Melissa Locker, "The Inane, Insane Insults World Leaders Have Hurled at Each Other," *Fast Company*, September 26, 2017.

35. Lawrence Friedman and Srinath Raghavan, "Coercion," in *Security Studies: An Introduction*, ed. Paul D. Williams and Matt McDonald (London: Routledge, 2018), 225.

36. Barbara Tuchman, *The March of Folly* (New York: Ballantine Books, 1984), 32.

37. Hannah Arendt, *The Origins of Totalitarianism* (New York: Harcourt, 196), vii.

38. US Department of Defense, *Summary of the National Defense Strategy of the United States* (Washington, DC, 2018), 2.

39. Ibid., 1.

40. Gregory D. Foster, "The National Defense Strategy Is No Strategy," *Defense One*, April 4, 2019.

41. Sweijs and Holstege, *Threats, Arms, and Conflicts*.

42. Joseph Nye, "Soft Power: The Origins and Political Progress of a Concept," *Palgrave Communications*, February 21, 2017.

43. Sweijs and Holstege, *Threats, Arms, and Conflicts*.

44. David Aucsmith, "A Theory of War in the Cyber Domain: Part 1, An Historical Perspective," Microsoft Institute for Advanced Technology in Government, March 5, 2012, 16.

45. National Defense Authorization Act for Fiscal Year 2019, Public Law 115-232, August 13, 2018.

46. Robert Chesney, "The Law of Military Operations and the New NDAA," *Lawfare*, July 26, 2018, www.lawfareblog.com/law-military-cyber-operations-and-new-ndaa.

47. Benjamin B. Hatch, "Defining a Class of Cyber Weapons as WMD: An Examination of the Merits," *Journal of Strategic Security* 11, no. 1 (2018): 44.

48. Martin C. Libicki, *Conquest in Cyberspace* (Cambridge: Cambridge University Press, 2007), 98.

49. US Department of Defense, *Nuclear Posture Review* (Washington, DC, 2018), 54.

50. Bruce W. MacDonald, "Deterrence and Crisis Stability in Space and Cyberspace," in *Anti-satellite Weapons, Deterrence, and Sino-American Space Relations*, ed. Michael Krepon and Julia Thompson (Washington, DC: Stimson Center, 2013), 84; Pavel Podvig and Hui Zhang, *Russian and Chinese Responses to U.S. Military Plans in Space* (Cambridge, MA: American Academy of Arts and Sciences, 2008), 31.

51. Valerie Insinna, "Air Force Leaders on Space Deterrence: At Some Point, We've Got to Hit Back," *Defense News*, April 16, 2019.

52. Richard Dempsey and Jonathan Chavous, "Commander's Intent and Concept of Operations," *Military Review*, November–December 2013.

53. Thomas Sarsfield, "Americans Aren't War Weary, They're War Apathetic," Modern War Institute, July 25, 2019, https://mwi.usma.edu/americans-arent-war-weary-theyre-war-apathetic/.

54. American Friends Service Committee, *Speak Truth to Power: A Quaker Search for an Alternative to Violence* (Philadelphia: American Friends Service Committee, 1955), quoted in David Cortright, *Peace: A History of Movements and Ideas* (Cambridge: Cambridge University Press, 2008), 124.

55. Tuchman, *March of Folly*, 374–77.

56. US Government Accountability Office, *Weapon System Cybersecurity*, GAO-19-128 (Washington, DC, 2019).

57. Neel V. Patel, "A Russian Satellite Is Probably Stalking a U.S. Spy Satellite in Orbit," *MIT Technology Review*, February 3, 2020.

58. Tim Hinchliffe, "In an Era of AI, You Need Human Intelligence: UK Spy Chief, " *The Sociable*, December 5, 2018.

59. Inga D. Neumann, Alexa H. Veenma, and Daniel I. Beiderbeck, "Aggression and Anxiety: Social Contexts and Neurobiological Links," *Frontiers in Behavioral Neuroscience* 4, no. 12 (2010), doi: 10.3389/fnbeh.2010.00012.

60. Sydney, J. Freedberg Jr., "Why a 'Human in The Loop' Can't Control AI: Richard Danzig," *Breaking Defense*, June 1, 2018.

61. Lucas Kello, "The Meaning of the Cyber Revolution: Perils to Theory and Statecraft," *International Security* 38, no. 2 (October 2013): 14.

62. Harold G. Moore and Joseph L. Galloway, *We Were Soldiers Once and Young* (New York: Random House, 1992).

63. Henry Kissinger, "How the Enlightenment Ends," *The Atlantic*, June 2018.

64. Adrian Poole, "The Force of Simone Weil on Homer," *Arion: A Journal of Humanities and the Classics* 2, no. 1 (Winter 1992): 6.

65. John Kester, "Hypersonic Missiles Could Trigger a War," *Foreign Policy*, October 2, 2017.

66. Heather Roff, "Banning and Regulating Autonomous Weapons," *Bulletin of the Atomic Scientists*, November 24, 2015.

FOUR. AVOIDING WAR

1. John F. Harris and Bryan Bender, "Bill Perry Is Terrified. Why Aren't You?," *Politico*, January 06, 2017.

2. Todd South, "Bringing Back the Draft," *Military Times*, July 25, 2017.

3. Samuel Moyn and Stephen Wertheim, "The Infinity War," *Washington Post*, December 15, 2019.

4. J. William Fulbright, *The Arrogance of Power* (New York: Vintage Books, 1966), 250, quoted in Jim Lobe, "The Arrogance of Power," *Foreign Policy in Focus*, September 1, 2002.

5. Giorgio Mariani, *Waging War on War: Peacefighting in American Literature* (Champaign: University of Illinois Press, 2015), xii.

6. Jake Sullivan, "What Donald Trump and Dick Cheney Got Wrong about America," *The Atlantic*, January/February 2019.

7. Robert H. Latiff, *Future War: Preparing for the New Global Battlefield* (New York: Knopf, 2017), 108.

8. Jimmy Carter, *The Words of Peace: Selections from the Speeches of the Winners of the Nobel Peace Prize*, ed. Irwin Abrams (New York: Newmarket Press, 2000), 86.

9. "The Cold War Is History. Now It's the Cool War" (editorial), *The Guardian*, February 23, 2013.

10. Andrew Bacevich, "8 Reasons Americans Can't Shake Their Indifference to War," *The Nation*, October 10, 2017.

11. Ann Bridges, review of *Future War: Preparing for the New Global Battlefield*, by Robert H. Latiff, Goodreads, November 10, 2017, www.good reads.com/review/show/2180288728.

12. Sissela Bok, *A Strategy for Peace* (New York: Pantheon Books, 1989), 145.

13. Timothy Snyder, *The Road to Unfreedom* (New York: Penguin Random House, 2018), 10.

14. David Brooks, "A Man on a Gray Horse," *The Atlantic*, September 1, 2002.

15. Sarsfield, "Americans Aren't War-Weary, They're War Apathetic," Modern War Institute, July 25, 2019, https://mwi.usma.edu/americans-arent -war-weary-theyre-war-apathetic/.

16. Craig Chamberlain, "Did News Coverage Turn Americans against the Vietnam War?," University of Illinois News Bureau, September 5, 2017; Michael Mandelbaum, "Vietnam: The Television War," *Daedalus* 111, no. 4 (Fall 1982): 157.

17. Lewis Mumford, "Gentlemen, You Are Mad!," *Maclean's*, June 1, 1946, quoted in H. Bruce Franklin, *War Stars: The Superweapon and the American Imagination* (Amherst: University of Massachusetts Press, 2008), 4.

18. S. Tagil, "Alfred Nobel's Thoughts about War and Peace," November 20, 1998, www.nobelprize.org/alfred-nobel/alfred-nobels-thoughts-about -war-and-peace/.

19. Julia Keller, "Mr. Gatling's Game Changing Gun," *Military History Quarterly* 22, no. 3 (2010): 10.

20. H. R. McMaster, "Crack in the Foundation," Strategy Research Paper, US Army War College, 2003, www.hsdl.org/?view&did=444508.

21. William A. Owens, *Lifting the Fog of War* (Baltimore: Johns Hopkins University Press, 2001), 14.

22. Mark Edele, "Fighting Russia's History Wars: Vladimir Putin and the Codification of World War II," *History and Memory* 29, no. 2 (Fall/Winter 2017): 106–7.

23. Suzanne Spaulding and Elizabeth Rindskopf-Parker, Statement before the National Commission on Military, National, and Public Service. Creating an Expectation of Service: Civic Education as a National Security Imperative," Washington, DC, July 10, 2019, www.inspire2serve.gov/_api/files/331.

24. Michael C. Desch, "The Relevance Question," in *Cult of the Irrelevant: The Waning Influence of Social Science in National Security,* ed. Michael C. Desch (Princeton, NJ: Princeton University Press, 2019), 2.

25. US Department of Veterans Affairs, "America's Wars Fact Sheet," November 2020, www.va.gov/opa/publications/factsheets/fs_americas_wars.pdf.

26. Neta Crawford, "Human Cost of the Post-9/11 Wars: Lethality and the Need for Transparency," Watson Institute Costs of War Project, Brown University, November 2018, https://watson.brown.edu/costsofwar/files/cow/imce /papers/2018/Human%20Costs%2C%20Nov%208%202018%20CoW.pdf.

27. Robin Wright, "What Would War with North Korea Look Like?," *New Yorker,* September 6, 2017.

28. Murtaza Hussain, "Why War with Iran Would Spell Disaster," Al Jazeera, September 12, 2012, www.aljazeera.com/indepth/opinion/2012/09 /201291194236970294.html.

29. "Substance Use Disorders among Military Populations," Butler Center for Research, Hazelden Betty Ford Foundation, May 2018, www.hazelden bettyford.org/education/bcr/addiction-research/substance-abuse-military -ru-518.

30. Stephen Losey, "Air Force Deaths by Suicide Spiked by One-Third in 2019," *Air Force Times,* January 31, 2020.

31. Dinah Walker, "Trends in U.S. Military Spending," Council on Foreign Relations, July 15, 2014, www.cfr.org/report/trends-us-military-spending.

32. Winslow Wheeler, "Correcting the Pentagon's Distorted Budget History," *Time* magazine, July 16, 2013.

33. US Congressional Research Service, "U.S. War Costs, Casualties, and Personnel Levels since 9/11," Report, IF11182, April 28, 2019, https:// crsreports.congress.gov/product/pdf/IF/IF11182/1.

34. "Economic Costs," Watson Institute Cost of War Project, Brown University, January 2020, https://watson.brown.edu/costsofwar/costs/economic.

35. "How Does The United States Military Budget Affect the Economy?," Wharton Public Policy Initiative, University of Pennsylvania, August 11, 2017, https://publicpolicy.wharton.upenn.edu/live/news/2046-how-does-the -united-states-military-budget-affect/for-students/blog/news.php.

36. Patrick Hiller, "The Effects of Military Spending on Economic Growth," *Peace Science Digest,* January 2, 2018, https://peacesciencedigest .org/effects-military-spending-economic-growth/.

37. "Where Do Our Federal Tax Dollars Go?," Policy Basics, Center on Budget and Policy Priorities, updated April 9, 2020, www.cbpp.org /research /federal-budget/policy-basics-where-do-our-federal-tax-dollars-go.

38. Dwight D. Eisenhower, "The Chance for Peace" speech, Washington, DC, April 16, 1953, https://millercenter.org/the-presidency/presidential-speeches/april-16-1953-chance-peace.

39. Hiller, "Effects of Military Spending."

40. "Economic Consequences of War," Institute for Economics and Peace, 2011, www.files.ethz.ch/isn/138799/DOWNLOAD-The-Economic-Consequences-of-War-on-the-US-Economy.pdf.

41. Stanley Waterloo, *Armageddon: A Tale of Love, War and Invention* (Chicago: Rand McNally, 1898), 251.

42. Willard M. Fox, "How to Finance a War," Foundation for Economic Education, July 1, 1966, https://fee.org/articles/how-to-finance-a-war/.

43. Adam J. Berinsky, "Assuming the Costs of War: Events, Elites, and American Public Support for Military Conflict," *Journal of Politics* 69, no. 4 (November 2007): 975.

44. "Americans' Knowledge of the Branches of Government Is Declining," Annenberg Public Policy Center, University of Pennsylvania, September 13, 2016, www.annenbergpublicpolicycenter.org/americans-knowledge-of-the-branches-of-government-is-declining/.

45. Jason Dempsey and Amy Schafer, "Is There Trouble Brewing for Civil-Military Relations in the U.S.?," *World Politics Review*, May 23, 2017.

46. Geoff Brumfiel, "U.S. Begins Production of a New Nuclear Weapon," NPR, January 31, 2109.

47. Kevin H. Wang, "Presidential Responses to Foreign Policy Crises," *Journal of Conflict Resolution* 40, no. 1 (March 1996): 69.

48. Charles W. Ostrom Jr. and Brian L. Job, "The President and the Political Use of Force," *American Political Science Review* 80, no. 2 (June 1986): 559.

49. Bradley Lian and John R. Oneal, "Presidents, the Use of Military Force, and Public Opinion," *Journal of Conflict Resolution* 37, no. 2 (June 1993): 277.

50. Paul L. Pillar, "Why Does America Inflate Threats from the Middle East?," *National Interest*, October 29, 2019.

51. Marvin Kalb, "What Was the Powell Doctrine?," excerpt from "The Road to War: Presidential Commitments Honored and Betrayed," lecture, October 2, 2013, Carnegie Council for Ethics in International Affairs, www.carnegiecouncil.org/education/008/expertclips/005.

52. Pew Research Center, "Partisan Differences in Views of Peace through Strength Grow Wider," October 4, 2017, www.people-press.org/2017/10/05/3-foreign-policy/3_4-13/.

53. James W. Carden, "Elizabeth Warren Has a Plan to Fix the State Department and No One Wants to Talk about It," *Quartz*, September 13, 2019.

54. Robbie Gramer and Colum Lynch, "Despite Pompeo's Call for Swagger, Trump Slashes Diplomatic Budget," *Foreign Policy*, March 11, 2019.

55. Qingsan Tan, "The Change of Public Opinion on U.S.-China Relations," *Asian Perspective* 35, no. 2 (Apr-June 2011): 222.

56. Eric Hyer, "Alternative Perspectives on U.S.-China Relations," in *The People's Republic of China Today: The Internal and External Challenges*, ed. Zhiqun Zhu (Singapore: World Scientific, 2011), 423.

57. Judy Dempsey, "NATO's European Allies Won't Fight for Article 5," *Carnegie Europe*, June 15, 2015, https://carnegieeurope.eu/strategiceurope /?fa=60389.

58. Peter Moore, "Ukraine: Little Support for U.S. Involvement," YouGov, March 3, 2014.

59. Molly J. Simis, Haley Madden, and Michael A. Cacciatore, "The Lure of Rationality: Why Does the Deficit Model Persist in Science Communication?," *Public Understanding of Science* 25, no. 4 (2016): 400–414. Research has shown that public communication is more complex than what the knowledge deficit model suggests. It assumes that public audiences can and do process information in a rational manner when in fact external factors play a large role and can often outweigh better knowledge as a factor in decision-making.

60. Members of the 2005 "Rising above the Gathering Storm" Committee, *Rising above the Gathering Storm, Revisited: Rapidly Approaching Category 5*, prepared for the presidents of the National Academy of Sciences, National Academy of Engineering, and Institute of Medicine (Washington, DC: National Academies Press, 2010).

61. National Commission on Military, National, and Public Service, *Inspired to Serve*, Final Report, March 2020, https://inspire2serve.gov/reports /final-report.

62. Association of American Colleges and Universities, *A Crucible Moment: College Learning and Democracy's Future*, National Task Force on Civic Learning and Democratic Engagement (Washington, DC: Association of American Colleges and Universities, 2012).

63. Roger P. Alfred, "The Nobel Effect: Nobel Peace Prize Laureates as International Norm Entrepreneurs," *Virginia Journal of International Law* 49, no. 1 (2008): 61.

64. Bertha von Suttner, *Lay Down Your Arms* (London: Longmans, Green, 1894), 432.

65. Jane Addams, *Newer Ideals of Peace* (New York: Macmillan, 1907).

66. Eric Arnesen, "Dissent and Disloyalty," *Chicago Tribune*, January 30, 2005.

67. Thomas Jefferson to John Taylor, June 1, 1798, in *The Works of Thomas Jefferson*, vol. 8, ed. Paul Leicester Ford (New York: G. P. Putnam's Sons, 1904), 432. See also Scott Horton, "Jefferson on the Reign of Witches," *Harper's Magazine*, July 4, 2007.

68. Geoffrey R. Stone, *Perilous Times: Free Speech in Wartime from the Sedition Act of 1798 to the War on Terrorism* (New York: W. W. Norton, 2004), 12.

69. David Kaiser, "The Atomic Secret in Red Hands? American Suspicions of Theoretical Physicists during the Early Cold War," *Representations* 90 (Spring 2005): 30.

70. Patrick David Slaney, "Eugene Rabinowitch, the Bulletin of the Atomic Scientists, and the Nature of Scientific Internationalism in the Early Cold War," *Historical Studies in the Natural Sciences* 42, no. 2 (April 2012): 132.

71. Rodney P. Carlisle and J. Geoffrey Golson, eds., *Turning Points—Actual and Alternate Histories: America in Revolt during the 1960s and 1970s* (Santa Barbara, CA: ABC-CLIO, 2008), 123–24.

72. Geoffrey Stone, "Dissent Is Not Disloyal," *Chicago Tribune*, December 24, 2004, 12.

73. Jerry Lembcke, *The Spitting Image: Myth, Memory, and the Legacy of Vietnam* (New York: New York University Press, 1998), 96.

74. Tim Pugmire, "Eugene McCarthy, Who Galvanized a Generation of War Opponents, Dies," Minnesota Public Radio, December 10, 2005.

75. Karen Zraick, "Greta Thunberg, after Pointed U.N. Speech, Faces Attacks from the Right," *New York Times*, September 24, 2019.

76. Charles Rabin, "Parkland Students Face New Attack, This Time from the Political Right on Social Media," *Miami Herald*, February 20, 2018.

77. Zachary Pleat, "Right-Wing Media Launch Unhinged Attacks on Greta Thunberg," *Media Matters*, September 24, 2019.

78. Rachel V. Kutz-Flamenbaum, "Code Pink, Raging Grannies, and Missile Dick Chicks: Feminist Performance Activism in the Contemporary Antiwar Movement," *NWSA Journal* 19, no. 1 (Spring 2007): 90.

79. Marie O'Reilly, "Why Women? Inclusive Security and Peaceful Societies," *Inclusive Security*, October 2015.

80. Danny Sjursen, "Where Are the Brave Military Voices against the Forever War?," *American Conservative*, September 19, 2017.

81. Samuel S. Kim, "The US Catholic Bishops and the Nuclear Crisis," *Journal of Peace Research* 22, no. 4 (1985): 321–33.

82. Gerald W. Schlabach, "Just War? Enough Already," *Commonweal*, May 31, 2017.

83. Reinhold Niebuhr, *Moral Man and Immoral Society* (Louisville, KY: Westminster John Knox Press, 2001), 87.

84. David S. Meyer, "How Social Movements Matter," *Contexts* 2, no. 4 (Fall 2003): 31.

85. David Cortright, *Peace: A History of Movements and Ideas* (Cambridge: Cambridge University Press, 2008), 175.

86. Alan Dawley, "Why Peace Movements Are Important," History News Network, May 8, 2006.

87. Phil Shannon, review of *A People's History of the Civil War: Struggles for the Meaning of Freedom*, by David Williams, *Green Left Weekly*, November 17, 1993.

88. Piero Gleijeses, "1898: Opposition to the Spanish-American War," *Journal of Latin American Studies* 35, no. 4 (November 2003): 706.

89. Milton C. Albrecht, "The Relationship of Literature and Society," *American Journal of Sociology* 59, no. 5 (March 1954): 425.

90. Moshin Hamid and Francine Prose, "Does Fiction Have the Power to Sway Politics?," *New York Times*, February 17, 2015.

91. Barbara Gold, "Simone Weil's Iliad: Misunderstanding Homer?," paper presented at 147th annual meeting of the Society for Classical Studies, January 2016.

92. Kurt A. Raaflaub, "Conceptualizing and Theorizing Peace in Ancient Greece," *Transactions of the American Philological Association* 139, no. 2 (Autumn 2009): 228.

93. Vera Brittain, Armistice Day article, *Manchester Guardian*, November 11, 1930, quoted in Charles Andrews, *Writing against War* (Evanston, IL: Northwestern University Press, 2017), 1.

94. Cynthia Wachtell, *War No More* (Baton Rouge: Louisiana State University Press, 2010), 6.

95. Tim O'Brien, "How to Tell a True War Story," in *The Things They Carried* (Boston: Mariner Books, 2009), 78.

96. Philip Caputo, *A Rumor of War* (New York: Ballantine Books, 1977); William Styron, "A Farewell to Arms," *New York Review of Books*, June 23, 1977.

97. Roy Scranton, *War Porn* (New York: Soho Press, 2017).

98. Michiko Kakutani, "*War Porn* Widens the Field of Vision about the Costs in Iraq," review of *War Porn*, by Roy Scranton, *New York Times*, August 8, 2016.

99. Jerrod Laber, "The Anti-war History of Literature," *New Liberal*, April 3, 2017.

100. Library of Congress, "Peace Songs of the Civil War," n.d., accessed January 30, 2021, www.loc.gov/item/ihas.200197667/.

101. Frankie Hill, "Songs of War: The Evolution of Protest Music in the United States," *Harvard Political Review*, March 14, 2016.

102. Lyn Smith, *Voices against War: A Century of Protest* (Edinburgh, UK: Mainstream, 2009), 77.

103. Pikria Saliashvili, "Music in War: From Rebellion to Patriotism," War on the Rocks, *Art of War* (blog), November 11, 2016, https://waronthe rocks.com/2016/11/music-in-war-from-rebellion-to-patriotism/.

104. Pete Seeger, "Where Have All the Flowers Gone?," on *Pete Seeger's Greatest Hits*, Columbia Records, CS 9416, 1967, LP Record.

105. Andrews, *Writing against War*, 198.

106. Pew Research Center, "Generational Differences Emerge in Views of Racial Discrimination, Equality," March 1, 2018, https://brewminate.com/the -generation-gap-in-american-politics/.

107. See "Generational Differences Chart, West Midland Family Center," n.d., accessed December 5, 2019, https://pdf4pro.com/view/generational -differences-chart-west-midland-family-center-46c272.html; Purdue University, "Generational Differences in the Workplace" (infographic), n.d., accessed December 5, 2019, www.purdueglobal. edu/education-partnerships/genera tional-workforce-differences-infographic/.

108. Pew Research Center, "Millennials: Confident, Connected, Open to Change," February 24, 2010, www.pewsocialtrends.org/2010/02/24/millen nials-confident-connected-open-to-change/.

109. Mary Miller, "Why Aren't More Young People Involved in the Anti-war Movement?," *Common Dreams*, November 1, 2018.

110. Yemi Babington-Ashaye, "What Do Young People Care About? We Asked 26,000 of Them," *World Economic Forum*, November 8, 2016.

111. Steve Cohen, "The Age Gap in Environmental Politics," *State of the Planet* (blog), Earth Institute, Columbia University, February 4, 2019, https:// blogs.ei.columbia.edu/2019/02/04/age-gap-environmental-politics/.

112. Larry Downes, *The Laws of Disruption: Harnessing the New Forces That Govern Life and Business in the Digital Age* (New York: Basic Books, 2009), 9.

113. Ben FitzGerald and Jacqueline Parziale, "As Technology Goes Demo-cratic, Nations Lose Military Control," *Bulletin of the Atomic Scientists* 73, no. 2 (2017): 102, http://dx.doi.org/10.1080/00963402.2017.1288445.

114. Ronald Arkin, Leslie Kaelbling, Stuart Russell, Dorsa Sadigh, Paul Scharre, Burt Selman, and Toby Walsh, "A Path towards Reasonable Autono-mous Weapons Regulation," *IEEE Spectrum*, October 21, 2019.

115. George Beebe, "We're More at Risk of Nuclear War with Russia Than We Think," *Politico*, October 7, 2019.

116. Zachary Davis and Michael Nacht, "Closing Thoughts: Humanity, Machines, and Power," in *Strategic Latency: Red, White, and Blue*, ed. Zachary S. Davis and Michael Nacht (Livermore, CA: Center for Global Security Research, Lawrence Livermore National Laboratory, 2018), 289.

117. Kenneth Anderson and Mathew C. Waxman., "Law and Ethics for Autonomous Weapon Systems: Why a Ban Won't Work and How the Laws of War Can," American University, Washington College of Law Research Paper 2013-11, April 10, 2013, https://ssrn.com/abstract=2250126 or http://dx.doi.org/10.2139/ssrn.2250126.

118. Paul Scharre, "Killer Apps: The Real Dangers of an AI Arms Race," *Foreign Affairs*, May/June 2019, https://omnilogos.com/killer-apps-real-dangers-of-ai-arms-race/.

119. David Montgomery, "A New Hope," *Washington Post Magazine*, December 8, 2019, 20.

120. Katrina van den Heuvel, "Why the New Cold War Is So Dangerous," *The Nation*, April 5, 2018.

121. Nicholas J. Wheeler, "The Priority of Trust in Signal Interpretation," in *Trusting Enemies: Interpersonal Relationships in International Conflict* (Oxford: Oxford University Press, 2018), 100–117.

122. Peter B. Zwack, "Pearl Harbor and the Fallacy of Inevitable War: The Thucydides Trap," *The Hill*, December 7, 2018.

123. Honoré de Balzac, "A Passion in the Desert," trans. Ernest Dowson (Adelaide: University of Adelaide Library, 2013), first published in 1830.

124. George C. Marshall, Nobel Peace Prize Acceptance Speech, December 11, 1953, www.nobelprize.org/prizes/peace/1953/marshall/acceptance-speech/.

125. Daniel May, "How to Revive the Peace Movement in the Trump Era," *The Nation*, March 16, 2017.

126. Daniel B. Kline, "Where Do Your Tax Dollars Actually Go?," *USA Today*, April 11, 2017.

127. Stephanie Savell, "The War on Apathy over America's Wars," *Salon*, February 25, 2018.

128. Jerrod A. Laber, "When We Raised Taxes to Fund Wars," *American Conservative*, July 12, 2018.

129. Anthony Everitt, *Cicero: The Life and Times of Rome's Greatest Politician* (New York: Random House, 2003), 12.

130. Frederick M. Barnard, "Patriotism and Citizenship in Rousseau: A Dual Theory of Public Willing?" *Review of Politics* 46, no. 2 (April 1984): 244–47.

131. Phillip Bump, "Millennials Embrace a Long-Standing Tradition: Letting Someone Else Fight Their Wars," *Washington Post,* December 10, 2015.

132. Everitt, *Cicero*, 17.

133. Amy Shafer, "The War on Apathy," *Slate*, October 31, 2017.

134. National Commission on Military, National, and Public Service, "Interim Report Executive Summary," January 23, 2019, www.inspire2serve .gov/FINAL%20Executive%20Summary.pdf.

135. Sarah Mervosh, "Will There Be a Draft? Young People Worry after Military Strike," *New York Times*, January 3, 2020.

CONCLUSION

1. Reinhold Niebuhr, *The World Crisis and American Responsibility*, ed. Ernest W. Lefever (New York: Association Press, 1958), 76, quoted in Andrew Bacevich, "Illusions of Managing History: The Enduring Relevance of Reinhold Niebuhr," *Historically Speaking*, January/February 2008.

INDEX

human control
  vs. artificial intelligence (AI),
    25–26, 27, 28, 29, 31–32,
    34–35, 134
  vs. automation, 12–13, 22–23,
    28, 32, 85
  and speed brakes, 8, 130–31
  and technological innovation,
    12–13, 23, 134
human migration, 49, 50, 51–52
human performance research, 14
Hungary
  Soviet invasion, 3
  US military in, 10
Hussain, Murtaza, 98–99
hybrid war, 4, 69–70
hypersonic weapons, 14, 15, 65,
    67–68, 76, 86, 137
hyperwar, 7, 13

IARPA (Intelligence Advanced
    Research Projects Activity),
    105
Industrial Revolution, 3
influential people, 109–15, 136
information technologies, 14–16,
    17, 94–95
  information warfare, 68, 94
intellectual property theft, 69
Intermediate Nuclear Forces (INF)
    Treaty, 122
international agreements, 121–22,
    123, 124, 137
international humanitarian law,
    123
internet-of-things, 15
Iran
  ballistic missiles of, 65, 67
  cyber weapons of, 69
  navy firing on own ship, 73

nuclear program, 65, 90, 98–99,
    105, 122, 123
  relations with United States, 64,
    75, 92, 98–99, 105, 122, 123,
    126, 129
  Stuxnet attack on centrifuges in,
    30
  US drone shot down by, 64
Iraq: US invasion and war in, 4, 7,
    65, 75, 81, 94, 98, 99, 104,
    114, 115, 116, 118
irrationality of war, 1–2
Israel: Syria attacked by, 6, 29, 90

Japan
  invasion of Manchuria, 50
  relations with China, 50
  relations with United States, 11,
    72
  US military in, 11
Jefferson, Thomas
  on "reign of witches," 112
  and USS *Chesapeake*, 5
Johnson-Freese, Joan: on space
    diplomacy, 123
Joint Comprehensive Plan of
    Action (JCPOA), 122
Joyce, Rob, 69
just war theory
  Aquinas and Augustine on, 114
  jus ad bellum (justice in going to
    war), 7
  jus in bello (justice in war), 7
JWICS (joint worldwide
    intelligence communications
    system), 12

Kalibr cruise missile, 72
Kant, Immanuel: "Perpetual Peace,"
    48

MAJOR GENERAL (RET.) ROBERT H. LATIFF

is adjunct professor with the John J. Reilly Center for Science, Technology, and Values at the University of Notre Dame and research professor at George Mason University. He is the author of *Future War: Preparing for the New Global Battlefield*.

Milton Keynes UK
Ingram Content Group UK Ltd.
UKHW051449020823
425933UK00029B/125